# Tales to Tickle Your Funny Bone

## *Humorous Tales from Around the World*

*Norma J. Livo*



*Foreword by Pat Mendoza*

A Member of the Greenwood Publishing Group

*Westport, Connecticut • London*

**Library of Congress Cataloging-in-Publication Data**

Livo, Norma J., 1929–
Tales to tickle your funny bone: humorous tales from around the world / Norma J. Livo.
p. cm.
Includes bibliographical references and index.
ISBN-13: 978-1-59158-504-6 (alk. paper)
1. Tales 2. Humorous stories. 3. Wit and humor. I. Title.
GR76.L58 2007
398.2–dc22 2007003331

British Library Cataloguing in Publication Data is available.



Library of Congress Catalog Card Number: 2007003331
ISBN-13: 978-1-59158-504-6

First published in 2007

Libraries Unlimited, 88 Post Road West, Westport, CT 06881
A Member of the Greenwood Publishing Group, Inc.
www.lu.com

Printed in the United States of America

The paper used in this book complies with the Permanent Paper Standard issued by the National Information Standards Organization (Z39.48–1984).

10 9 8 7 6 5 4 3 2 1

*To my children Lauren Joan, Keith Eric, Kim Bruce, and Robert Craig, who have literally saved my life as well as constantly enriched it.*

# *Contents*

# *Foreword*

Norma Livo has always made me laugh. When I first met her over twenty years ago, she gave me a bumper sticker that she had created. It read: "Old Storytellers Never Die, They Simply Lose Their Tales." That is when I knew this PhD had not only an incredible mind, but also a great sense of humor. She had just contracted me, sight-unseen, to be a keynote performer for the Rocky Mountain Storytelling Festival. She had heard of my work and felt as she said, "The conference needed me."

Ever since that first meeting, I have been awed by her knowledge, her generosity, and her wit. She is one of the true raconteurs in the storytelling world. Jimmy Neil Smith, the founder of the National Storytelling Festival in Jonesborough, Tennessee affectionately calls Norma, "the Grand Dame of Western Storytelling." Norma still loves people and collects stories whenever and wherever she can from the people and culture that told them. And, there is always a funny story in her waiting to come out.

During those early years, Norma organized the Rocky Mountain Storytelling Conference through the University of Colorado at Denver. She brought participants from the western states the likes of Garvin Taylor, an old time cowboy whose father had purchased the Kaycee Ranch in Wyoming from the outlaw Butch Cassidy. Garvin was one of the funniest people I have ever known. I have performed stand-up comedy and heard many in the business, but none of them could make me laugh like Garvin could. Garvin is only one example of the hundreds of people Norma has presented to the world of story lovers. Another was the late Sam Arnold, the owner of the Fort Restaurant. He regaled listeners with his stories of the bear Sissy, he took care of for years as well as old western recipes and the stories behind them. Sam was another of those people whose humor was natural and appealing. Through Norma, I got to know both of these incredible men.

For the past thirty-one years, I have made my full-time living as a storyteller and folk singer. Like Norma, I like to observe people and places. One of the things I always look for are signs of intelligence, the lack thereof and most importantly, a sense of humor. For example, a few years ago, as I was driving into the small South Dakota town of Gettysburg, I noticed the official town limits sign that read, "Welcome to Gettysburg, South Dakota… Where the Battle Wasn't." That's when I knew the folks there had a great sense of humor and I wasn't disappointed.

Everybody in every culture laughs (unless that person is a total psychopath) and in this book *Tales to Tickle Your Funny Bone: Humorous Tales from Around the World*, Norma proves just that. From Finland to Scotland to ancient Greece and India, to Asia, Africa, England and Ireland, and then into the Carolinas and the American West, these stories are examples that laughter is spoken fluently throughout the world.

What Norma has compiled in this collection are classic and untold humorous stories that range from Aesop's fables to the very funny and unexpected endings of some of the stories. At the same time, Norma hasn't forgotten her native western Pennsylvanian roots and the story her father told about… well read it as I did, you'll love it. Norma also retells some of the tales that were told by mountain men and travelers like Jim Bridger and others like him. The people of the east didn't believe their observations of the incredible scenery of the west. Out of this some of our country's classic tall tales were born.

Norma Livo, "the Grande Dame of Western Storytelling" has done it again, and through this book she has made me laugh with every turn of every page.

Pat Mendoza<br>
An American Troubadour<br>
Denver, Colorado

# *Introduction*

*There are three things which are real: God, human folly, and laughter. The first two are beyond our comprehension. So we must do what we can with the third.*

*John F. Kennedy*

It may seem simple, but humor is a complex and powerful human experience that we all have from time to time, but few of us understand. As human beings, we enjoy humor; but what is funny to one person may not be funny to the next. As a storyteller, I can tell you that humor can be a great tool for breaking the ice with strangers, for grabbing your audience's attention, for defusing a tense situation, for giving listeners insight into their behaviors, and for teaching us about ourselves.

This collection of humorous tales and riddles is meant to supply you with a wide assortment of funny stories from all over the world that you can use, add to your storytelling repertoire, or read aloud in the classroom, library, board room, or at home. The stories are grouped according to type. "The Foolish, the Clever, and the Wise" contains those tales that come to us through the long tradition of folklore. Here you'll find sad princesses, clever girls, foolish boys, strong boys, and many silly animals among other characters. But foolishness rises to another level when experienced in a group, as we see in the next section, "Noodleheads." And then there are always those characters bent on making fools of others—"Tricksters," such as Anansi the spider from Africa, Tyll Ulenspiegel of Belgium, and the Persian Nasruddin. "Tall Tales" is a form of exaggeration that rises to a humorous level. We also find humor in "Family Stories, Local Legends, Hoaxes, and Urban Myths." Think about your own family stories, and you'll likely remember a few that are often shared to solicit chuckles. Words can delight us too, and this is the type of humor you'll find in the final category, "Riddles, Verses, Rhymes, and Songs."

Unless otherwise indicated, the stories in this collection come from my own repertoire as a storyteller. I have made an effort to find tales from a variety of cultures and countries, although some categories are dominated by stories from particular areas of the world. For example, although there are ancient predecessors to tall tales, this form of stories came into its own on American soil, particularly the American frontier; and thus, this is the one section where stories from the United States predominate.

As fun as it is on its own, humor can be put to much good use. It can heal, it can bring us together, and it can teach. Let's take a closer look at some of the applications of humor that might help us as storytellers, educators, and parents.

## HEALING POWER OF HUMOR

Stories heal our spirits by helping us laugh. Health professionals have even begun to accept the value of mirth as a vital force in physical care and recovery. For example, clowns, humor carts, funny books, comics and videos, and humor rooms are available in hospitals for the patients.

Many health professionals believe that humor creates positive cognitive changes and relieves stress. Some suggest that mirthful laughter is actually a form of physical therapy. How? Among the benefits of laughter are providing exercise by increasing the heart rate, stimulating blood circulation and breathing, and improving muscle tone.

It is calculated that one hundred laughs equal ten minutes of working on a rowing machine. In *Anatomy of an Illness as Perceived by the Patient* (New York: W.W. Norton, 1979), Norman Cousins refers to laughter as "inner jogging." Several studies have shown that laughing lessens the need for medication and shortens recuperation time. It even reduces pain, serving as the body's natural painkiller.

Humor also serves to reduce stress by lowering levels of cortisol, a stress hormone that can weaken the immune system. Who would believe that laughing also stimulates the immune system and regulates cell growth? Doctors who use humor soon discover that it also builds a closer relationship with their patients and can serve as a preventive medicine.

The Flying McCoys, July 31, 2006, by Gary McCoy.

Many medical professionals use humor for their patients and among themselves. There is a great deal of humor that focuses on medicine and the medical world. For instance: HAZMAT teams are highly trained professionals, not "glow worms." Another quick medical quip: "Tell me doctor, how much time do I have left to live?" The doctor's answer, "Well, it's hard to say, but if I were you, I wouldn't start watching any serials on TV."

The handwriting of physicians on prescriptions has been another source of professional humor: "Doctors at a hospital in Brooklyn, New York, have gone on strike. Hospital officials say they will find out what the doctors' demands are as soon as they can get a pharmacist over there to read the picket signs."

## THE SOCIAL POWER OF HUMOR

Laughter also serves as a social tool. A quote from Alan Alda fits here. "When people are laughing, they are generally not killing each other." Further than that, in human relations, humor is often our best defense. A humorous approach can often defuse an angry verbal attack. When someone accused Lincoln of being "two-faced," he quickly replied, "If I really did have another face, do you think I'd still wear this one?"

Many Egyptian jokes are highly political such as in the 1960s when Abdel Nasser's government created problems for people in everyday life. Nasser became furious at the fun being made of him and ordered the person making the jokes to be brought to him.

"Are you the one who made up these jokes?" he asked the man.

"Yes," was the prompt reply.

"Did you start this joke? And this one?" Nasser continued.

The prompt reply was "yes."

Nasser then drew himself up into a commanding stance and demanded, "Don't you know that I was elected by 99.8% of the people?"

"Oh, no" came the reply, "I'm not responsible for that joke."

One Egyptian sociologist claims that humor is a sort of defense mechanism. "We are able to make fun of our leaders, of ourselves, of our problems. It enables us to cope with a lot."

Folklore is not only old and dare we say, ancient, but it is also existing in our contemporary lives and historical time period. Bumper stickers are one current example and source of humor:

- *Out of my mind. Back in five minutes.*
- *Give me ambiguity or give me something else.*
- *He who laughs last, thinks slowest.*

Before bumper stickers, there was Burma-Shave! I venture that many children were motivated to read during the 1950s as they traveled in the family car. Before the Internet, Burma-Shave signs were posted along the road. There were usually five or six signs spaced along the road. They contained such gems as:

*Cattle crossing*
*Means go slow*

*That old bull*
*Is some*
*Cow's beau*
*Burma-Shave*

*His crop of*
*Whiskers*
*Needed reaping*
*That's what kept*
*His Lena leaping*
*Burma-Shave*

*Don't*
*Try passing*
*On a slope*
*Unless you have*
*A periscope*
*Burma-Shave*

*Passing cars*
*When you can't see*
*May get you*
*A glimpse*
*Of eternity*
*Burma-Shave*

*Many a forest*
*Used to stand*
*Where a*
*Lighted match*
*Got out of hand*
*Burma-Shave*

*On curves ahead*
*Remember sonny*
*That rabbit's foot*
*Didn't save*
*The bunny*
*Burma-Shave*

## THE TEACHING POWER OF HUMOR

Among the most important tools to enhance education that a teacher has are humorous stories which encourage imagination and creativity in so many ways. One of the recent complaints heard from youngsters is that there is too much homework. Perhaps assignments involving stories and humor can entice our students to new discoveries.

Activities involving stories with humor might be a welcome replacement to commercial worksheets in homework assignments. Humor is also something which can involve youngsters and their families as well as other community members, and maybe kick up some good old memories along with smiles.

This collection of humorous stories can be used at all levels of our educational system. Its assortment of stories and ideas just might be the spark your youngsters respond to. All areas of the curriculum, reading, writing, oral literature, language development, social science, and mathematics, are richer if a touch of humor is added to it.

Humor may be sly, slapstick, subtle, or warm. We may find humor in the dialogue and the use of words or exaggeration. Word play and wit can be quite sophisticated. There are also puns, which cause many people to groan and grimace while others laugh. I know of some punsters who have developed this form of humor to an art form. Humor can be thought of as comedy, jests, jokes, satire, and whatever else induces laughter. Royal courts of old had their jesters who were retained to amuse the royalty and their court. The jester also assumed aspects of the fool when entertaining.

### Activity Possibilities

Just as humor has been found to help maintain and improve our health, the same goes for our mental functions such as alertness and memory. Many activities involving humor can be used in educational settings. Many of the following activity ideas fit school, library, family, or other community groups. Consider these possibilities:

- *Obtain some digital cameras. Send youngsters home with cameras with instructions to take photographs they can find in their environments that demonstrate and capture humor. Share them with the group.*
- *After youngsters share their pictures, print, mount, and label them in a class book of "humor" for a resource in the classroom library.*
- *Have the youngsters share true stories and events from their lives that illustrate humor.*

- *Instruct them to keep a journal of funny happenings and sights they discover in their school for a period of one week.*
- *Discuss with the youngsters humor that is funny and humor that may hurt a person. Have them brainstorm ways to discourage others from using hurtful humor.*
- *The following cartoon,* Cornered, *by Mike Baldwin, refers to the possibility that humor shouldn't be analyzed too much. Have the youngsters discuss what this means and give some examples.*
- *Have the youngsters draw or photograph funny faces. Then, have them choose one and write a story about what happened before and after the funny face was made.*
- *Instruct the youngsters to keep a log of the times they laughed during one day. What was it that made them laugh? Have them share their notes and list how many were similar in content and how many were different.*
- *In a small group, brainstorm why funny stories are important. Make a list of these ideas.*
- *Many stories, ballads, and riddles come from a variety of cultures. Every cultural group throughout the world has its own assortment of characters and stories, so search them out and familiarize yourself with the*

Humor is everywhere. As we travel, I look for humor and find it. For instance, this forlorn figure sits on the filling station island beside the gasoline pump in Scotland. Photograph by Norma J. Livo.

We all know scarecrows, don't we? Here is a scarecrow found in a garden in Scotland. What might a scarecrow in China look like? Photograph by Norma J. Livo.

*geographical locations of the stories. (I once had a graduate student make the appalling confession that she "didn't have a culture," considering an ethnic background as the only possibility of culture. Since she was an assimilated American, she figured she had no roots to count on.)*

- *Many humorous stories are drawn from American folklore and legends. Provide a map of the United States. As you read and discover folklore and legends from the United States with the youngsters, locate their place of origin on the map, and add the titles along with pertinent captions. Key the items to the map. Write a paragraph summary of each item. For example, Oklahoma is part of Cherokee history. The Cherokee story of how fire came to earth was told by its former inhabitants. A raven could be placed on the map as a symbol and the story included in a booklet to explain each symbol.*
- *On a map of the United Sates, ask youngsters where they would locate these characters: Barney Beal, Bowleg Bill, Moby Dick, Blackbeard, Ichabod Crane, Gib Morgan, John Henry, Joe Magarac, Paul Bunyan, Casey Jones, John Chapman, Davy Crockett, Mike Fink, Jean Lafitte, Tom Sawyer, Wild Bill Hickok, Febold Feboldson, Pecos Bill, Calamity Jane, Jim Bridger, Jedediah Smith, William Cory, Finn MacCool, Kit Carson, Sam McGee, and Annie Christmas.*
- *Weather is a natural topic for tall tales, and a whopper category of funny stories. Use the following to provide ammunition for a contest in writing a whopper.*

  *It was so hot that ..................................................*
  *It was so cold that ..................................................*
  *It was so windy that ..............................................*
  *It was so dry that ..................................................*
  *It was so wet that ..................................................*
- *Interview some older folks and ask them to tell you about the most extreme weather they can recall. Collect these stories along with details about the person giving you the story, where it happened, and how that person felt during that time. These stories could be compiled into a "Weather of Our Lives" booklet.*
- *Choose a ballad or poem and rewrite it as a story.*
- *Ask youngsters what the difference is between telling a lie and telling a whopper. Has any one ever told a lie to you? How did that make you feel?*
- *Develop one of the whopper stories into a readers theater script or some creative dramatic activities.*
- *Research riddles that you discover from many places. Keep them in a folder until you have enough to develop a booklet of riddles of the world.*

*Share this with friends, family, and cohorts, and ask them if they have any additional riddles to contribute.*

- *Youngsters could choose one of the stories from this collection and develop it into a puppet show. Create music to go along with it. Have them present this show for friends, family, or other groups.*
- *Have the youngsters investigate local urban legends in their area. Compile a collection of them.*
- *Youngsters could collect variants of any of the stories in this book by researching in the library and on the Internet. Use the different versions to study how the details, settings, and events have been changed, and write an essay on why these differences may have occurred.*
- *Have youngsters choose one of the stories that interests them and alter it to create a new story to share. Think of the settings and characters and substitute others to develop their own story.*
- *Explore "noodlehead" stories. Discuss what they liked or disliked in these stories with others. Ask them, "Why do you think these stories were created?"*
- *For youngsters, the story "The Hummingbird" might remind them that many times older people might consider them and their thinking as "being just like a kid" or "too young to help out." Brainstorm some ways that youngsters can get involved and help out. Read the newspaper and see how many instances of young people coming to the rescue are reported.*
- *Create humorous bumper sticker slogans or posters.*
- *Develop a crossword puzzle involving humor and humorous characters.*
- *Have youngsters illustrate one of the stories in this book using one of a variety of media, such as pastels, chalk, oil or acrylic paints, clay, or collage. Or create the story in comic book form. Make a display of these around the classroom.*
- *After reading the stories, ask youngsters to make a chart that compares and contrasts two of them. Examine the themes, characters, and settings.*
- *Have youngsters write a sequel to one of the stories.*
- *Have youngsters illustrate one of the stories with a series of drawings. Cut the pictures apart, write the sequence number on the back of each one, and then mix them up. Tell the story to someone. Then give that person your pictures and have them place the pictures in the correct order. When they are done, have them use the sequence numbers on the back to self-check the order.*
- *In the story "Dull or Noodle," the character's answers surprise and unsettle the listeners. Challenge youngsters to develop a list of clever answers or responses that would surprise listeners and turn around their (maybe) cruel remarks and questions that may have hurtful intentions.*

- *Interview miners to discover any beliefs they learned or heard about in the mining industry. Keep a dictionary of mining vocabulary.*
- *Have youngsters interview people from their community who were not born in the United States; and collect stories and beliefs from their native countries.*
- *Ask youngsters to investigate occupations, such as carpenters, accountants, and teachers, to see if there are any superstitions, humorous elements, myths, or practical jokes involved in them.*
- *Have youngsters interview older folks such as friends, relatives, or possibly people in a nursing home, and collect any local stories they know. These stories could be published or exhibited in a display. Ask a librarian to share any of the "Foxfire" material cited in the bibliography with you.*
- *Investigate with youngsters some of the beliefs and legends related to flowers. For instance, how did forget-me-nots get their name?*
- *Discuss why the great scientist Albert Einstein prescribed, "Fairy tales, more fairy tales and more fairy tales" as the way to develop imagination. Can you create a new folktale or tall tale for your community?*
- *After reading the story "Truth?" ask the youngsters to respond. Discuss this story with others and compare reactions to it.*
- *Have youngsters review some of the stories and find a character they would like for a friend. Ask them to write or talk about their qualities and why they would want them for a friend.*
- *Have youngsters reflect on a personal or family memory that contains humor; then develop it into a story, write it, and tell it. What worked? What didn't work? Why?*
- *Have youngsters share the above stories with family or friends. Then ask them if their family members' memories differed from theirs. How? Why?*
- *This personal or family memory can also be written and presented as a play. At a family gathering, select family members to read the parts and present the play.*
- *"The Secret Life of Walter Mitty" is a classic piece of humorous writing. Its author, James Thurber, is acknowledged as the greatest American humorist since Mark Twain. Read Thurber's story of Walter Mitty along with some of his other writings. He wrote several books for children that were prize-winners. Also, study some of his cartoons. Humor anyone?*
- *Mary McDonough Coyle Chase was awarded the Pulitzer Prize for her play* Harvey. *Hoping to bring laughter to wartime America, she wrote her play influenced by stories she had heard as a child.* Harvey, *her 6 foot 1½ inch imaginary white rabbit, was based on the* pooka, *a trickster creature of Irish folklore.* Harvey *was such a success that it went on to be a blockbuster movie starring Jimmy Stewart. Obtain*

*copies of the play or movie and enjoy sessions of reading the play and examining its humor.*

- *Have youngsters cut four photographs from newspapers or magazines, or bring in unrelated actual photographs—preferably not "head shots." Place them in an order and then write a story based on them. Describe what happened first, next, and at the end. Mount them on poster board and include their original story of them.*
- *Have youngsters select a current product being advertised, or invent their own, and write 5 Burma Shave-style rhymes using their product. Then, have them draw a picture of a curving road and place the rhymes on the passenger-side of the road. Share this with others.*
- *And finally, ask youngsters, "Why do you think the author took the photograph below as an example of something that made her laugh?"*

The educational possibilities of humor are truly endless. If you work with youngsters, let yourself go, add to this list of possibilities, and keep a record of your efforts. Which ideas worked, didn't work, or inspired new ideas? However you use this book, it is my hope that along with the serious endeavors of teaching and healing, you also get a few laughs of your own.

This photograph gives us a humorous look at a little drummer boy in a Scottish pipe and drum group. Photograph by Norma J. Livo.

# *Why Everyone Should Be Able to Tell a Story*

(Scotland)

Many years ago in Scotland, it was common for a traveler to try to relax when the convenience of going from the mainland to the islands wasn't as peaceful and easy as it is today. For instance, in those days, travelers whose destination was the island of Uist in the Outer Hebrides, used to come by the Isle of Skye. They crossed by boat from Dunvegan to Lochmaddy.

It happened that during these former times, a Uist fellow, Ian McKissack, who had been working the harvest on the mainland, was on his way home. Ian had worked hard that season and was eager to get back home to his family. He was walking through Skye one evening as the gloaming announced the coming of nightfall.

Ian came to a house and thought that since he had such a long way yet to go, he would stay there till morning. Ian called out "hello" to the house, and the man of the house came to the door. He made Ian welcome, and asked him to come in and join the family for some tea and scones.

As they sat in the kitchen warmed by a peat fire, the host asked Ian, "Have you any tales or stories to share with us this evening?" Ian put his cup of tea down, frowned and replied, "Well now, I have never known any."

The whole family looked at Ian in surprise, from the young bairns to their grandfather. "What! Never known any stories? That is very strange that you can't remember or tell a story," muttered Ian's host. "I'm sure that you must have heard plenty of them as you were growing up."

"Well, sad to say, I can't remember even one if I did indeed hear any," Ian answered. He sat quietly at the table and ran his hand through his red hair. "No, I really don't know any."

For the rest of the evening and into the night, Ian's host and his family told one story after another. Quietly one of the children would go outside to the pile of peat when the fire died down and bring in several slabs to add to the fire. Telling stories was what they did to pass the night until it was time go to bed. Ian thought to himself that this had been a most pleasant way to spend the evening.

Ian was given the room inside the front door to sleep in. The family kept their coats, boots and other outside-gear stored in the room. Off in one corner of this room was the carcass of a sheep, hanging to season, but the cot Ian slept on was cozy and clean.

Ian had not been in bed but a short time when he heard the door to the room open quietly and in the light of the moon, he saw two men come in and take the sheep from where it was hanging and slip outside. They didn't bother to close the door.

"How will I explain what just happened?" Ian said to himself as he sat up in his bed. "If I let those two men take the sheep, what will the host and his family think happened? They might even think that I wanted the sheep and hid it somewhere."

He slipped into his clothes and went after the thieves. He wasn't too quiet as he followed them and one of them heard him, looked back and saw him following them. In a gruff voice, the thief said, "Look at that fellow coming after us. He could turn us in. Let's catch him and make sure he won't be able to identify and tell on us."

They dropped the sheep, turned back and took off after Ian. Ian knew if they caught him he was in for trouble, so he turned and tried to get back to the house and sound an alarm. He wasn't fast enough because the two thieves got between him and the house. Ian kept running for all he was worth, until he heard the sound of a big river. "Quick feet, get me to the river," he thought as he ran.

Now in a panic, Ian went straight into the river. The rushing stream carried him away. "Oh no! Now I might drown," he thought. Thrashing around, he got hold of a branch of a tree that was growing on the bank of the river. He frantically clung to it, too frightened to move. He heard the two thieves going back and forth along the banks of the river looking for him. They were throwing stones wherever the trees cast their shadows. Some of the stones passed right over his head.

And so, this man from Uist, only wanting to get home again, remained hanging on to the tree branch until dawn. It had been a frosty night and when Ian tried to get out of the river, he just couldn't do it. His cold muscles didn't seem to work. He slipped and slid and stirred the water into a mucky condition around him. He tried to shout for help, but he couldn't shout either. His voice just didn't work. Only his teeth made noise as they chattered. At last, he managed to utter one feeble cry. At the same time, he took a tentative leap, landed in a patch of nettles, and woke up.

There he was on the floor beside the bed, holding on to the bedclothes with both hands. Ian's host had been on his mind during the night! In the morning as they were all eating a warm breakfast of oatmeal, he told his host of what he had dreamed during the night.

"Well, I am sure that wherever you are tonight, you will have a story to tell even though you didn't have one last evening," said the host. And as he said that, he leaned back in his chair and laughed.

So that is what happened to the man who couldn't tell a story. It all just goes to prove that everyone should be able to tell a tale, sing a song, or tell a story to help pass the evening!

# *The Foolish, the Clever, and the Wise: Stories from Folklore*

*Humor is the shock absorber of life; it helps us take the blows*

*Peggy Noonan*

# *Lazy Jack*

(England)

Once upon a time, there was a boy whose name was Jack. He lived with his mother on a small farm. Now, Jack and his mother were very poor. The old woman earned money by spinning, but her son Jack was so lazy that he would do nothing but bask in the sun on sunny days and sit close to the corner of the fireplace in the winter. That, of course, was why people called him Lazy Jack. His mother could not get him to do anything at all around the farm. She had reached the end of her rope of patience one Monday when she told Jack that if he did not begin to work and help out, there would be not any more porridge for him. In fact, she told him, "I will turn you out to get your own living any way that you can."

This threat caught Jack's attention, and he went out and found work the next day with a neighboring farmer for a penny. After work, as he was coming home, whistling, he was very careless with his money and lost it in the water of a brook.

"I have never had money before, mother. I did not know what to do with it," he told his mother that evening.

His mother moaned, "You stupid boy! You should have put the money in your pocket to carry it home."

"Next time, that is exactly what I will do mother," Jack told her.

Jack went out again on Wednesday and got work with a cow-keeper. When the workday was over, the cow-keeper gave Jack a jar of milk in payment for his day's work. Remembering what his mother told him, Jack put the jar into the large pocket of his jacket. Naturally, it all spilled long before he got home.

"Son!" scolded his old mother. "You should have carried the jar of milk on your head."

"I'll remember that next time mother," Jack said.

Thursday came and Jack went back to the farmer and found work. This time, Jack was paid with cream cheese for his day's efforts. At the end of the day, Jack took the cheese and took off for home with the cheese on his head. By the time he got home, the cheese was all spoiled, some of it had been lost and some of it was matted into his hair.

"You ridiculous fellow!" cried his mother. "You should have carried it very carefully in your hands."

"Yes mother. I will do so the next time," replied Jack.

On Friday, Lazy Jack went out again and found work with a baker. This time, the baker paid him for his work with a large tom-cat. Jack took the cat, and remembering what his mother had said, carried it very carefully in his hands. In a short time the cat scratched and clawed him so much that he was forced to let it go.

When he got home, his mother heard his story and told him, "You silly fellow. You should have tied it with a string and dragged it along behind you."

"Yes mother," Jack said. "I will remember to do that the next time."

On Saturday, Jack found work with the butcher. After a full day of work, the butcher paid Jack by giving him a shoulder of mutton. Jack found some string and tied it to the mutton. Then he dragged the shoulder of mutton along after him in the dirt. By the time he got home, the meat was completely spoiled. His mother who saw this was completely horrified.

"Tomorrow is Sunday and all we have to eat will be cabbage. How good the mutton would have been!" she complained. And so they ate cabbage for dinner.

"You ninnyhammer," she complained to her son. "How could you have destroyed the shoulder of mutton? You should have carried it on your own shoulder."

"Yes, mother. I will do that very thing the next time," agreed Jack.

On Monday, Lazy Jack went out once more and found work with a cattle-keeper. At the end of the long dusty day of work, the cattle-keeper gave Jack a donkey in payment. Jack worked hard to hoist the donkey on his shoulders and somehow, at last, he managed it. So, he trudged slowly toward home with his reward for the day.

Along his route home, there lived a rich man with his only daughter. She was a beautiful girl but was not able to hear or speak. Besides that, she had never laughed once in her life. The doctors told her father that she would never be able to speak until something made her laugh.

This lovely girl was looking out of the window just as Jack was passing by with the squirming donkey on his shoulders. The legs of the donkey were sticking up straight in the air. The sight was so comical and strange that the girl burst into a great fit of laughter. And just as the doctors had said, she immediately recovered her speech and hearing. Her father was overjoyed, and remembered that he had promised that anyone who could make his daughter laugh would win her hand in marriage.

The rich man was so happy that he told Lazy Jack, "You have just won my daughter in marriage. You have done what no others could do. She laughed and was miraculously healed."

Of course, Jack became a rich man and lived with his new wife in a fine large house. In fact, Jack's mother lived with them in great happiness until the day she died.

# *The Bee, the Harp, the Mouse, and the Bum-Clock*

(Ireland)

Once there was a widow, and she had one son, called Jack. Jack and his mother owned just three cows. They lived well and happy for a long time; but at last hard times came down on them, the crops failed, and poverty looked in at the door. Things got so sore against the poor widow that for want of money and for want of necessities she had to make up her mind to sell one of the cows. "Jack," she said one night, "go over in the morning to the fair to sell the branny (speckled brown) cow."

Well and good. In the morning my brave Jack was up early, and took a stick in his fist and turned out the cow, and off to the fair he went with her; and when Jack came into the fair, he saw a great crowd gathered in a ring in the street. He went into the crowd to see what they were looking at, and there in the middle of them he saw a man with a wee, wee harp; a mouse; a bum-clock (cockroach); and a bee to play the harp. And when the man put them down on the ground and whistled, the bee began to play the harp, and the mouse and the bum-clock stood up on their hind legs and got hold of each other and began to waltz. And as soon as the harp began to play and the mouse and the bum-clock to dance, there wasn't a man or woman or a thing in the fair that didn't begin to dance also, and the pots and pans and the wheels and reels jumped and jiggled all over the town, and Jack himself and the branny cow were as bad as the next.

There was never a town in such a state before or since, and after a while the man picked up the bee, the harp, the mouse, and the bum-clock and put them into his pocket, and the men and women, Jack and the cow, the pots and pans, and wheels and reels that had hopped and jigged now stopped, and everyone began to laugh as if to break his heart.

Then the man turned to Jack, "Jack," says he, "how would you like to be master of all these animals?"

"Why," says Jack, "I should like it fine."

"Well, then," says the man, "how will you and me make a bargain about them?"

"I have no money," says Jack.

"But you have a fine cow," says the man. "I will give you the bee and the harp for it."

"Oh, but," Jack says, says he, "my poor mother at home is very sad and sorrowful entirely, and I have this cow to sell and lift her heart again."

"And better than this she cannot get," says the man. "For when she sees the bee play the harp, she will laugh as she never laughed in her life before."

"Well," says Jack, says he, "that will be grand."

So Jack made the bargain. The man took the cow, and Jack started home with the bee and the harp in his pocket, and when he came home, his mother welcomed him back.

"And Jack," says she, "I see you have sold the cow."

"I have done that," says Jack.

"Did you do well?" says the mother.

"I did well, and very well," says Jack.

"How much did you get for her?" says the mother.

"Oh," says he, "it was not for money at all I sold her, but for something far better."

"Oh, Jack! Jack!" says she, "what have you done?"

"Just wait until you see, Mother," says he, "and you will soon say I have done very well."

Out of his pocket he took the bee and the harp and set them in the middle of the floor, and whistled to them, and as soon as he did this, the bee began to play the harp. The mother she looked at them and let a big, great laugh out of her, and she and Jack began to dance. The pots and pans, the wheels and reels began to jig and dance over the floor, and the house itself hopped about also.

When Jack picked up the bee and the harp again, the dancing all stopped, and the mother laughed for a long time. But when she came to herself, she got very angry entirely with Jack, and she told him he was a silly, foolish fellow, and that there was neither food nor money in the house, and now he had lost one of her good cows, also.

"We must do something to live," says she. "Over to the fair you must go tomorrow morning, and take the black cow with you and sell her."

And off in the morning at an early hour, brave Jack started, and never halted until he was in the fair. When he came into the fair, he saw a big crowd gathered in a ring in the street. Said Jack to himself, "I wonder what they are looking at."

Into the crowd he pushed, and saw the wee man this day again with a mouse and a bum-clock, and he put them down in the street and whistled. The mouse and the bum-clock stood up on their hind legs and got hold of each other and began to dance there and jig, and as they did there was not a man or woman in the street who didn't begin to jig also, and Jack and the black cow and the wheels and the reels and the pots and pans, all of them were jigging and dancing all over the town, and the houses themselves were jumping and hopping about, and such a place Jack or anyone else never saw before.

When the man lifted the mouse and the bum-clock into his pocket, they all stopped dancing and settled down, and everybody laughed right hearty. The man turned to Jack.

"Jack," said he, "I am glad to see you; how would you like to have these animals?"

"I should like well to have them," says Jack, says he, "only I cannot."

"Why cannot you?" says the man.

"Oh," says Jack, says he, "I have no money, and my poor mother is very downhearted. She sent me to the fair to sell this cow and bring some money to lift her heart."

"Oh," says the man, says he, "if you want to lift your mother's heart I will sell you the mouse and when you set the bee to play the harp and the mouse to dance to it, your mother will laugh as she never laughed in her life before."

"But I have no money," says Jack, says he, "to buy your mouse."

"I don't mind," says the man, says he, "I will take your cow for it."

Poor Jack was so taken with the mouse and had his mind so set on it, that he thought it was a grand bargain entirely, and he gave the man his cow, and took the mouse and started off for home, and when he got home his mother welcomed him.

"Jack," says she, "I see you have sold the cow."

"I did that," says Jack.

"Did you sell her well?" says she.

"Very well indeed," says Jack, says he.

"How much did you get for her?"

"I didn't get any money," says he, "but I got value."

"Oh, Jack, Jack!" says she, "what do you mean?"

"I will soon show you that mother," says he, taking the mouse out of his pocket and the harp and the bee and setting all on the floor; and when he began to whistle, the bee began to play, and the mouse got up on its hind legs and began to dance and jig, and the mother gave such a hearty laugh as she never laughed in her life before. She set to dancing and jigging herself and Jack fell, and the pots and pans and the wheels and reels began to dance and jig over the floor, and the house jigged also. And when they were tired of this, Jack lifted the harp and the mouse and the bee and put them in his pocket, and his mother she laughed for a long time.

But when she got over that she got very downhearted and very angry entirely with Jack.

"And oh, Jack," she says, "you are a stupid, good-for-nothing fellow. We have neither money nor meat in the house, and here you have lost two of my good cows, and I have only one left now. Tomorrow morning," she says, "you must be up early and take this cow to the fair and sell her. See to get something to lift my heart up."

"I will do that," says Jack, says he. So he went to his bed, and early in the morning he was up and turned out the spotty cow and went to the fair.

When Jack got to the fair, he saw a crowd gathered in a ring in the street.

"I wonder what they are looking at, anyhow," says he. He pushed through the crowd, and there he saw the same wee man he had seen before with a bum-clock; and when he put the bum-clock on the ground, he whistled, and the bum-clock began to dance, and the men, women, and children in the street, and Jack and the spotty cow began to dance and jig also, and everything on the street and about it, the wheels and reels, the pots and pans, began to jig, and the houses themselves began to dance likewise. And when the man lifted the bum-clock and put it in his pocket, everybody stopped jigging and dancing and everyone laughed loud. The wee man turned and saw Jack.

"Jack, my brave boy," says he, "you will never be right fixed until you have this bum-clock, for it is a very fancy thing to have."

"Oh, but," says Jack, says he, "I have no money."

"No matter for that," says the man, "you have a cow, and that is as good as money to me."

"Well," says Jack, "I have a poor mother who is very downhearted at home, and she sent me to the fair to sell this cow and raise some money and lift her heart."

"Oh, but Jack," says the wee man, "this bum-clock is the very thing to lift her heart, for when you put down your harp and bee and mouse on the floor, and put the bum-clock along with them, she will laugh as she never laughed in her life before."

"Well, that is surely true," says Jack, says he, "and I think I will make a swap with you."

So Jack gave the cow to the man and took the bum-clock himself, and started for home.

His mother was glad to see Jack back, and says she, "Jack, I see that you have sold the cow."

"I did that, Mother," says Jack.

"Did you sell her well, Jack?" says the mother.

"Very well indeed, Mother," says Jack.

"How much did you get for her?" says the mother.

"I didn't take any money for her, Mother, but value," says Jack, and he takes out of his pocket the bum-clock and the mouse, and set them on the floor and began to whistle, and the bee began to play the harp and the mouse and the bum-clock stood up on their hind legs and began to dance, and Jack's mother laughed very hearty, and everything in the house, the wheels and the reels, and the pots and pans, went jigging and hopping over the floor, and the house itself went jigging and hopping about likewise.

When Jack lifted up the animals and put them in his pocket, everything stopped, and the mother laughed for a good while. But after a while, when she came to herself, and saw what Jack had done and how they were now without either money, or food, or a cow, she got very, very angry at Jack, and scolded him hard, and then sat down and began to cry.

Poor Jack, when he looked at himself, confessed that he was a stupid fool entirely.

"And what," says he, "shall I now do for my poor mother?"

He went out along the road, thinking and thinking, and he met a wee woman who said, "Good-morrow to you, Jack," says she, "how is it you are not trying for the king's daughter of Ireland?"

"What do you mean?" says Jack.

Says she, "Didn't you hear what the whole world has heard, that the king of Ireland has a daughter who hasn't laughed for seven years, and he has promised to give her in marriage, and to give the kingdom along with her, to any man who will take three laughs out of her."

"If that is so," says Jack, says he, "it is not here I should be."

Back to the house he went, and gathers together the bee, the harp, the mouse, and the bum-clock, and putting them into his pocket, he bade his mother good-bye, and told her it wouldn't be long till she got good news from him, and off he hurried.

When he reached the castle, there was a ring of spikes all round the castle and men's heads on nearly every spike there.

"What heads are these?" Jack asked one of the king's soldiers.

"Any man that comes here trying to win the king's daughter, and fails to make her laugh three times, loses his head, and has it stuck on a spike. These are the heads of the men that failed," says he.

"A mighty big crowd," says Jack, says he. Then Jack sent word to tell the king's daughter and the king that there was a new man who had come to win her.

In a very little time the king and the king's daughter and the king's court all came out and sat themselves down on gold and silver chairs in front of the castle, and ordered Jack to be brought in until he should have his trial. Jack, before he went, took out of his pocket the bee, the harp, the mouse, and the bum-clock, and he gave the harp to the bee, and he tied a string to one and the other, and took the end of the string himself and marched into the castle yard before all the court, with his animals coming on a string behind him.

When the queen and the king and the court and the princes saw poor, ragged Jack with his bee and mouse and bum-clock hopping behind him on a string, they set up one roar of laughter that was long and loud enough. And when the king's daughter herself lifted her head and looked to see what they were laughing at, and saw Jack and his paraphernalia, she opened her mouth and she let out of her such a laugh as was never heard before.

Then Jack drops a low curtsy and says, "Thank you, my lady; I have one of the three parts of you won."

Then he drew up his animals in a circle, and began to whistle, and the minute he did, the bee began to play the harp, and the mouse and the bum-clock stood up on their hind legs, got hold of each other, and began to dance, and the king and the king's court and Jack himself began to dance and jig, and everything about the king's castle, pots and pans, wheels and reels, and the castle itself began to dance also. And the king's daughter, when she saw this, opened her mouth again, and let out of her a laugh twice louder than she let before; and Jack, in the middle of his jigging, drops another curtsy, and says, "Thank you, my lady; that is two of the three parts of you won."

Jack and his menagerie went on playing and dancing, but Jack could not get the third laugh out of the king's daughter, and the poor fellow saw his big head in danger of going on the spike. Then the brave mouse came to Jack's help; and wheeled round upon its heel, and as it did so its tail swiped into the bum-clock's mouth, and the bum-clock began to cough and cough and cough. And when the king's daughter saw this she opened her mouth again, and she let the loudest and hardest and merriest laugh that was ever heard before or since; and, "Thank you my lady," says Jack, dropping another curtsy; "I have all of you won."

Then when Jack stopped his menagerie, the king took him and the menagerie within the castle. He was washed and combed, and dressed in a suit of silk and satin, with all kinds of gold and silver ornaments, and then was led before the king's daughter. And true enough, she confessed that a handsomer and finer fellow than Jack she had never seen and she was very willing to be his wife.

Jack sent for his poor old mother and brought her to the wedding, which lasted nine days and nine nights, every night better than the other. All the lords and ladies and gentry of Ireland were at the wedding. I was at it too, and got brogues, broth, and slivers of bread and came jiggling home on my head.

*From* Troubadour's Storybag, *edited and retold by Norma J. Livo (Golden, CO: Fulcrum, 1996).*

# *Fat or Lean*

(Virginia, United States)

Do you know any old folks with rheumatism? Well, this story is about an old man who was crippled up with rheumatism. He hadn't walked a step for twelve years. Imagine that, not walked a step for twelve long years!

Most of the time he just sat on the front porch in a big rocking chair. It was full of quilts to soften it. Family had to carry him in to put him to bed every night. He was resigned to the fact that he would probably never be able to walk again. He had even heard the doctor tell his family that in all likelihood, he would never be able to walk again. He hadn't seen anyone with rheumatism this bad.

One day, he was sitting in his chair all bent over, gently rocking. The chair squeaked as he rocked. A young fellow saw him there on the porch and stopped to talk with the old man.

"What do you know about the house down a ways that no one has lived in for several years?" he asked. "I have heard folks talking about it being haunted. They say that nobody would stay in it even one night."

"Ain't nothing to it," said the old man. "Why, I'd stay all night in it just to prove to you that there is no problem. That is, if I could get down there."

"I have an idea," mused the boy. "Will you go there and stay with me? I could carry you there on my back."

"Sure I would go," answered the old man, "if you could get me there." They talked some more and decided to go that very night.

Well, it happened that there were two rascals who had come into that settlement on the same day. They made a plan to steal a sheep that night and cook it and as coincidences go, they planned to cook it in that same old house.

One of them planned to steal the sheep. He told the other fellow to meet him at that house. The second man even stole some meal and salt, went down to the old house where he gathered enough wood to roast the sheep. After all this, he was tired so he climbed up into the loft and laid down. The floor up there was rough since some of the boards were broken and loose but he got himself a place to lay down all fixed up. From where he was he could watch for his friend with the sheep.

About that time, the boy came along carrying the old man on his back. They went on into the house and when the rascal in the loft saw them, he thought that it was his buddy carrying the sheep. He stuck his head down into the room and asked, "Is he fat?"

The boy threw the old man on the floor and hollered up, "Fat or lean, you can have him!" He took off out of the house and down the road as hard as he could go. When he got to some houses, he slowed down a little and what did he see? There on the porch was the crippled old man sitting on the front porch rocking away as usual.

The old man called out to the boy, "What in heaven took you so long to get away from the house?" After that night, the old man was never bothered with rheumatism any more!

# *The Sad Princess*

(Norway)

Back in the days, over two hundred years ago, there was a king who had a wonderful kingdom, over which he ruled with virtue and peace. His problem was that he had a daughter. His problem was not how she looked, because she was so lovely that the reports of her beauty traveled far and wide. Then what was the problem? Alas, she was so melancholy that she never smiled let alone laughed. Along with that, she was so grand and proud that she said, "No," to all the handsome young men who came especially to woo her. She would not have any of them, even if they were ever so fine, whether they were prince or of noble birth.

The king grew tired of her attitude and decided his daughter ought to get married just like other people. There was nothing holding her back, no need to wait until she was old enough and she would not be any richer either, for she was to have half the kingdom, which she would inherit after her mother passed away.

So, the king made known every Sunday after the service, from the steps outside the church, that he who could make his daughter laugh should have both her and half the kingdom. But if there was anyone who tried and could not make her laugh, he would have three red stripes cut out of his back and then salt rubbed into them. It is very sad to relate that there were many sore backs in that kingdom.

Would-be lovers from south and from north, from east and from west, came to try their luck. They thought it was an easy thing to make a princess laugh. One man juggled, and another made strange faces. Yet another told jokes and funny stories. Altogether, they were a queer lot. However, for all of their cleverness and for all the tricks and pranks they played, the princess remained as serious and immovable as ever.

It happened that close to the palace, there lived a man who had three sons, and they eventually heard about the king's proclamation that he who could make the princess laugh should have her and her riches.

The eldest of the brothers wanted to try first, and away he went. When he came to the palace, he told the king he wanted to try and make the princess laugh.

"Yes, yes! That's all very well," said the king, "but I am afraid it's of very little use, my young man. There have been many here to try their luck, but my daughter is just as sad as ever. It's no good trying. I do not want to see any more suffer on my daughter's account."

But the lad decided he would try anyway. It couldn't be such a difficult thing to make a princess laugh at him. Had not everybody, both grand and simple, laughed so many times at him when he served as soldier and went through his drill under Sergeant Nils?

So he went out on the terrace outside the princess's windows and began drilling just as if Sergeant Nils himself were there. Oh, but it was all in vain! The princess sat as serious and immovable as before. So the king's men took him and cut three broad red stripes out of his back, rubbed salt into them and sent him home.

The oldest son had no sooner arrived home than his younger brother wanted to set out and try his luck. The second son was a schoolmaster, and an altogether funny figure he was. He had one leg shorter than the other and limped terribly when he walked. One moment he was no bigger than a boy, but the next moment, when he raised himself up on his long leg, he was as big and tall as a giant. Besides all that, he was great at preaching.

When he came to the palace and said that he wanted to make the princess laugh, the king thought it not so unlikely that he might. "But I pity you if you don't succeed," said the king, "for we cut the stripes broader and broader for every suitor that tries."

The schoolmaster went out on the terrace and took his place outside the princess's window. He began preaching and chanting, imitating seven of the parsons, and at the same time he was reading and singing just like seven of the clerks whom they had had in the parish.

The king laughed at the schoolmaster till he was obliged to hold on to the doorpost, and the princess was just on the point of smiling. But suddenly she was as sad and immovable as ever. So, it fared no better with Paul, the schoolmaster than with Peter, the soldier, for Peter and Paul were their names, you must know!

The king's men took Paul and cut three red stripes out of his back, put salt into them, and sent him home.

Well, the youngest brother, John, thought he would have a try next. John's older brothers laughed and made fun of him and showed him their sore backs. Besides, the father would not let him go, he said it was no use his trying.

"You have so little sense," the father told John. "All you can do is sit in a corner on the hearth like a cat, rooting about in the ashes and cutting chips." But John would not give in. He begged, he prayed, he begged some more, then he prayed even more until they got sick and tired of his whimpering. Finally his father granted him leave to go to the king's palace and try his luck.

When he arrived at the palace, John did not say he had come to try to make the princess laugh, but asked if he could get a job there at the castle. No, they had no work for him. John was not so easily put off, "You might want someone to carry wood and water for the kitchen maid in such a big palace as this," he said. The king finally agreed. To get rid of the lad, he gave him permission to remain there and carry wood and water for the kitchen maid. One day when he was going to fetch water from the brook, John saw a big fish in the water just under an old root of a fir tree from which the current had carried all the soil away. He put his bucket quietly under the fish and caught it. As he was going home to the palace, he met an old woman leading a golden goose.

"Good day, grandmother!" said John. "That is a fine bird you have there. It has such splendid feathers, too! I could see him shining from a long way off. If one had such feathers, one needn't be chopping firewood."

The woman thought just as much of the fish that John had in the bucket so she said, "If you give me the fish, you may have the golden goose. But let me warn you that this goose is such that if any one touches it, he will stick fast to it. You only need to say, 'If you'll come along, then hang on.'"

Yes, John would willingly exchange on those terms. "A bird is as good as a fish any day," he said to himself. "If it is as you say, I might use it instead of a fish hook," he told the woman. He was greatly pleased with owning the goose.

John had not gone far before he met another old woman. When she saw the splendid golden goose, she just had to go up to it and stroke it. She made herself so friendly and spoke so nicely to John. "May I stroke that lovely golden goose of yours?" she asked.

"Oh, yes!" said John, "but you must not pluck off any of its feathers!"

Just as she stroked the bird, John said, "If you'll come along, then hang on!"

The woman pulled and tore, but she had to hang on whether she liked it or not. John walked on as if he only had the goose with him.

When he had gone some distance, he met a man who had spite against the woman for a trick she had played upon him. When he saw that she fought so hard to get free and seemed to hang on so fast, he thought he might safely venture to pay her off for the grudge he owed her. He gave the woman a kick!

"If you'll come along, then hang on!" said John, and the man was stuck. He had to limp along on one leg whether he liked it or not. When he tried to tear himself loose, he made it still worse for himself for he was very nearly falling on his back whenever he struggled to get free.

So on they went until they came in the neighborhood of the palace. There they met the king's smith. He was on his way to the smithy and had a large pair of tongs in his hand. This smith was a merry fellow and was always full of mad pranks and tricks. When he saw this procession coming jumping and limping along, he began laughing till he was bent in two.

Suddenly he said, "This must be a new flock of geese for the princess. Who can tell which is goose and which is gander? I suppose it must be the gander toddling on in front. Goosey, goosey!" he called and pretended to be strewing corn out of his hands as when feeding geese.

But the procession did not stop. The woman and the man only glared furiously at the smith for making fun of them. The smith said, "It would be great fun to see if I could stop the whole flock, many as they are!" Now, he was a very strong man and he seized the old man with his tongs from behind in his trousers.

The man shouted and struggled hard, but John said, "If you'll come along, then hang on!"

With that, the smith was stuck, too. He bent his back and stuck his heels in the ground when they went up a hill and tried to get away but it was of no use. He hung on to the others as if he had been screwed fast in the great vice in the smithy. Whether he liked it or not, he had to dance along with the others.

When the group came near the palace, the farm dog ran against them and barked at them as if they were a gang of tramps. The princess came to look out of her window to see what the matter was and saw the strange procession. She burst out laughing. John was not satisfied with that, "Just wait a bit. She will laugh still louder very soon," he said and made a tour around the palace with his followers.

When they came past the kitchen, the door was open and the cook was just boiling porridge. When she saw John and his train after him, she rushed out the door with the porridge spoon in one hand and a big ladle full of boiling porridge in the other. She laughed till her sides shook. When she saw the smith there as well, she thought she could have burst with laughter. After she had a regular good laugh, she looked at the golden goose again and thought it was so lovely that she must stroke it.

"John, John!" she cried and ran after him with the ladle in her hand. "Just let me stroke that lovely bird of yours."

"Rather let her stroke me!" said the smith.

"Very well," said John.

But when the cook heard this, she got very angry. "What is it you say?" she cried. As she said this, she gave the smith a smack with the ladle.

"If you'll come along, then hang on!" said John and so she stuck fast to the others too. For all her scolding and all her tearing and pulling, she had to limp along with all the others.

The group stumbled past the princess's window again, and she was still there waiting for them. When she saw that they had got hold of the cook too, with the ladle and porridge spoon, she laughed till the king had to hold her up.

So, that's how John got the princess and half of the kingdom. They had a wedding that was heard of far and wide. Even his arrogant older brothers, who had once treated John with such disrespect, came to the wedding. When the princess smiled at John, they knew that he would have no red stripes down his back with salt in them. They also knew that the princess was no longer sad.

# *The Clever Cook*

(Germany)

There was once a cook called Gretel, who wore shoes with red heels; and when she went out in them she gave herself great airs, and thought herself very fine indeed. When she came home again, she would take a drink of wine to refresh herself, and as that gave her an appetite, she would take some of the best of whatever she was cooking, until she had had enough for, said she, "a cook must know how things taste."

It happened that one day her master came to her and said, "Gretel, I expect a guest this evening. You must make ready a pair of fowls."

"I will see to it," answered Gretel.

So she killed the fowls, cleaned them, and plucked them, and put them on the spit, and then, as evening drew near, placed them before the fire to roast. When they began to be brown, and were nearly done, the guest was still absent.

"If he does not make haste," cried Gretel to her master, "I must take them away from the fire. It's a pity and a shame not to eat them now, just when they are done to a turn."

The master said, "I will run myself and fetch the guest."

As soon as he had turned his back, Gretel took the fowls from before the fire.

"Standing so long before the fire," said she, "makes one hot and thirsty and who knows when they will come! In the meanwhile I will go to the cellar and have a drink." So down she ran, took up a mug, and saying, "Here's to me!" took a good draught. "One good drink deserves another," she said, "and it should not be cut short," so she took another hearty draught. Then she went and put the fowls down to the fire again, and basting them with butter, she turned the spit briskly around. And now they began to smell so good that Gretel said, "I must find out whether they really are all right," licked her fingers and then cried, "well I never! The fowls are good. It's a sin and a shame that no one is here to eat them!"

So she ran to the window to see if her master and his guest were coming, but as she could see nobody she went back to her fowls. "Why, one of the wings is burning!" she cried presently, "I had better eat it and get it out of the way." So she cut it off and ate it up, and it tasted good, and then she thought, "I had better cut off the other too, in case the master should miss anything." When both wings had been disposed of, she went and looked for the master, but still he did not come.

"Who knows," said she, "whether they are coming or not? They may have put up at an inn." After a pause she said again, "Come, I may as well make myself happy, and first I will make sure of a good drink and then of a good meal. When all is done I shall be easy. The gifts of the gods are not to be despised." So, first she ran down into the cellar and had a wonderful drink, and ate up one of the fowls with great relish. When that was done, and still the master did not come, Gretel eyed the other fowl, saying, "What one is the other must be, the two belong to each other. It is only fair that they should be both treated alike. Perhaps when I have had another drink, I shall be able to manage it." So, she took another hearty drink, and then the second fowl went the way of the first.

Just as she was in the middle of it, the master came back. "Make haste Gretel," cried he. "The guest is coming directly!"

"Very well, master," she answered. "It will soon be ready."

The master went to see that the table was properly laid, and taking the great carving knife with which he meant to carve the fowls, he sharpened it upon the step. Presently came the guest, knocking very genteelly and softly at the front door. Gretel ran and looked to see who it was and when she caught sight of the guest she put her finger on her lip saying, "Hush! Make the best haste you can out of this, for if my master catches you, it will be bad for you. He asked you to come to supper, but he really means to cut off your ears! Just listen how he is sharpening his knife!"

The guest, hearing the noise of the sharpening, made off as fast as he could go. And Gretel ran screaming to her master. "A pretty guest you have asked to the house!" she cried.

"How so, Gretel? What do you mean?" he asked.

"What indeed!" said she. "Why he has gone and run away with my pair of fowls that I had just dished up."

"That's pretty nasty sort of conduct indeed!" said the master, feeling very sorry about the fowls. "He might at least have left me one, that I might have had something to eat." And he called out to the guest to stop. But the guest made as if he did not hear him. Then the master ran after him, the knife still in his hand, crying out, "Only one! Only one!" meaning that the guest should let him have one of the fowls and not take both. The guest thought he meant to have only one of his ears, and so he ran much faster so that he might get home with both of his ears safely attached to his head.

# *Clever Else*

(Germany)

There was once a man who had a daughter who was called "Clever Else," and when she was grown up, her father said she must be married.

Her mother said, "Yes, if we could only find some one that she would consent to have."

At last one came from a distance, and his name was Hans, and when he proposed to her, he made it a condition that Clever Else should be very careful as well as lovely.

"Oh," said the father, "she does not want for brains."

"No, indeed," said the mother, "she can see the wind coming up the street and hear the flies cough."

"Well," said Hans, "if she does not turn out to be careful too, I will not have her."

Now when they were all seated at the table and had eaten very well, the mother said, "Else, go into the cellar and draw some beer."

Then Clever Else took down the jug from the hook in the wall, and as she was on her way to the cellar she rattled the lid up and down so as to pass away the time. When she got there, she took a stool and stood it in front of the cask, so that she need not stoop and make her back ache with needless trouble. Then she put the jug under the tap and turned it, and while the beer was running, in order that her eyes should not be idle, she glanced hither and thither, and finally caught sight of a pickaxe that the workmen had left sticking in the ceiling just above her head.

Then Clever Else began to cry for she thought, "If I marry Hans, and we have a child, and it grows big, and we send it into the cellar to draw beer, that pickaxe might fall on its head and kill it." So there she sat and cried with all her might, lamenting the anticipated misfortune.

All the while they were waiting upstairs for something to drink, and they waited in vain. At last the mistress said to the maid, "Go down to the cellar and see why Else does not come."

So the maid went, and found her sitting in front of the cask crying with all her might. "What are you crying for?" said the maid.

"Oh dear me," answered Clever Else, "how can I help crying? If I marry Hans, and we have a child, and it grows big, and we send it here to draw beer, perhaps the pickaxe may fall on its head and kill it."

"Our Else is clever indeed!" said the maid, and directly sat down to bewail the anticipated fortune.

After a while, when the people upstairs found that the maid did not return, and they were becoming more and more thirsty, the master said to the boy, "You go down into the cellar, and see what Else and the maid are doing."

The boy did so, and there he found both Clever Else and the maid sitting crying together. Then he asked what was the matter.

"Oh dear me," said Else, "how can we help crying? If I marry Hans and we have a child and it grows big and we send it here to draw beer, the pickaxe might fall on its head and kill it."

"Our Else is clever indeed!" said the boy and sitting down beside her, he began howling with a good will.

Upstairs they were all waiting for him to come back but as he did not come, the master said to the mistress, "You go down to the cellar and see what Else is doing."

So the mistress went down and found all three in great lamentation and when she asked the cause, then Else told her how the future possible child might be killed as soon as it was big enough to be sent to draw beer, with the pickaxe falling on it. Then the mother at once exclaimed, "Our Else is clever indeed!" and, sitting down, she wept with the rest.

Upstairs the husband waited a little while, but as his wife did not return, and as his thirst constantly increased, he said, "I must go down to the cellar myself, and see what has become of Else."

And when he came into the cellar and found them all sitting and weeping together, he was told that it was all owing to the child that Else might possibly have, and the possibility of its being killed by the pickaxe so happening to fall just at the time the child might be sitting underneath it drawing beer. When he heard all this, he cried, "How clever is our Else!" and sitting down, he joined his tears to theirs.

The intended bridegroom stayed upstairs by himself a long time, but as nobody came back to him, he thought he would go himself and see what they were all about. And there he found all five lamenting and crying most pitifully, each one louder than the other. "What misfortune has happened?" cried he.

"Oh my dear Hans," said Else, "if we marry and have a child and it grows big and we send it down here to draw beer, perhaps that pickaxe which has been left sticking up there might fall down on the child's head and kill it. How can we help crying at that?"

"Now," said Hans, "I cannot think that greater sense than that could be wanted in my household, so as you are so clever Else, I will have you for my wife." He took her by the hand and led her upstairs. They held their wedding at once.

A little while after they were married, Hans said to his wife, "I am going out to work, in order to get money. Go into the field and cut the corn so that we may have bread."

"Very well, I will do so dear Hans," said she.

After Hans was gone she cooked herself some nice stew and took it with her into the field. When she got there, she said to herself, "Now, what shall I do? Shall I reap first, or eat first? All right, I will eat first."

Then she ate her fill of stew and when she could eat no more, she said to herself, "Now, what shall I do? Shall I reap first, or sleep first? All right, I will sleep first." Then she lay down in the corn and went to sleep.

When Hans got home, he waited there a long while and Else did not come so he said to himself, "My Clever Else is so industrious that she never thinks of coming home and eating."

But when evening drew near and still she did not come, Hans set out to see how much corn she had cut. She had cut no corn at all, but there she was lying in it asleep. Then, Hans made haste home and fetched a bird-net with little bells and threw it over her. Still she went on sleeping. He ran home again and locked himself in and sat down on his bench to work.

At last, when it was beginning to grow dark, Clever Else woke up. When she got up and shook herself the bells jingled at each movement that she made. Then she grew frightened and began to doubt whether she were really Clever Else or not. She said to herself, "Am I, or am I not?" Not knowing what answer to make, she stood for a long while considering. At last she thought, "I will go home to Hans and ask him if I am or not. He is sure to know."

She ran up to the door of her house but it was locked. She knocked at the window and cried, "Hans, is Else within?"

"Yes," answered Hans. "She is in."

Then she was in a greater fright than ever and cried, "Oh dear, then I am not I." She went off to inquire at another door but the people hearing the jingling of the bells would not open to her. She could get in nowhere. So she ran away beyond the village and since then no one has seen her.

*Collected by the Brothers Grimm.*

# *A Wolf in Sheep Clothing*

(Greece)

A certain wolf, being very hungry, disguised himself in a sheep's skin and joined a flock of sheep. In this way, for many days he could kill and eat sheep whenever he was hungry. Even the shepherd did not find him out in his disguise.

One night after the shepherd had put all his sheep in the fold, he decided to kill one of his own flock for food. Without realizing what he was doing, he took out the wolf and killed him on the spot.

It really does not pay to pretend to be what you are not.

*Story told by Aesop.*

# *The Fox and the Crow*

(Greece)

A fox once saw a crow making off with a piece of cheese in its beak and made up his mind that he was going to get that cheese. "Good morning, friend crow," he called. "I see your feathers are as black and shiny and beautiful as ever. They gleam and glisten and change color as you move. You really are a beautiful bird. It is just such a shame that your voice is poor! If it were lovely like your feathers, you would, without question be the ruler of the birds."

The crow, was indignant that the fox doubted the beauty of her voice. Just to show fox how beautiful her voice was, crow began to caw at once. First softly and then raucously with her head thrown back. Of course as she cawed and moved her head, the cheese dropped.

Fox put his paw on the cheese and yelled, "I have what I wanted. Let me give you a bit of advice—don't trust flatterers."

*Story told by Aesop.*

# *The Miller, His Son and the Ass*

(Greece)

A miller and his son were driving an ass to the market to sell it. Some young people passing by made fun of them for walking when the ass might be carrying one of them. Upon hearing their remarks, the father had the boy get on the ass and was walking along quite happily until an old man met them. "You lazy rascal," he called to the boy. "You ride and let your poor old father walk!"

The son, turned red-faced with shame and quickly climbed off the ass and insisted that his father ride. Not long after this, they met another man who cried out to them, "How selfish that father is, to ride and let his young son walk!"

At that, the miller took his son up on the ass with himself, thinking he had at last done the right thing. But alas, he hadn't, for the next person they met was more critical than the others. "You should be ashamed of yourself," he said. "To have both of you riding that poor little beast! You are much better able to carry it."

Discouraged but willing to do right, the miller and his son got off the ass, bound its legs together on a long pole, and thus carried it on to the market. When they entered town, however, they made such a funny sight that crowds gathered about them laughing and shouting.

This noise frightened the ass so much that he kicked himself free and tumbled into the nearby river and was drowned.

The disgusted miller called to his son, “Come along.” With that, the two of them rushed back home.

“Well,” said the father, “we have lost the ass, but we have learned one thing—that when one tries to please everybody, he pleases none. Not even himself.”

*Story told by Aesop.*

# *The Wisdom of Hodja*

(Persia)

When they asked the wise Hodja how he acquired his great wisdom with questions like, "Who was your teacher?" "Where did you go to study?" "What writings were most important to you?" the wise Hodja sat and thought before he gave them his answer.

"When I hear that somebody has wisdom, I go and listen to what they have to say. If I see that people are listening to me, I try to find out afterwards what I just said," he quietly answered.

# *The Emperor's New Clothes*

(Sweden)

*This is a retelling of a well-known Swedish tale, written by a famous author, Hans Christian Andersen.*

Many years ago there lived an emperor who thought so much of new clothes that he spent all his money in order that he might be very fine. He did not care for his soldiers, nor for going to the play, or driving in the park, except to show his new clothes. He had a coat for every hour of the day, and just as they say of a king, "He is in the council-room," so they always said of him, "The Emperor is in his dressing-room."

The great city where he lived was very gay; and every day many strangers came there. One day there came two swindlers; they gave out that they were weavers, and said they could weave the finest cloth to be imagined. Their colors and patterns, they said, were not only exceptionally beautiful, but the clothes made of their material possessed the wonderful quality of being invisible to any man who was unfit for his office or hopelessly stupid.

"Those must be wonderful clothes," said the Emperor. "If I wore such clothes I should be able to find out which men in my empire were unfit for their places, and I could tell the clever from the stupid. Yes, I must have this cloth woven for me without delay." And he gave a lot of money to the two swindlers in advance, so that they should set to work at once. They set up two looms, and pretended to be very hard at work, but they had nothing whatever on the looms. They asked for the finest silk and the most precious gold; which they put in their own bags, and worked at the empty looms till late into the night.

"I should very much like to know how they are getting on with the cloth," thought the Emperor. But he felt rather uneasy when he remembered that he who was not fit for his office could not see it. He believed, of course, that he had nothing to fear for himself, yet he thought he would send somebody else first to see how matters stood. Everybody in the town knew what a wonderful property the stuff possessed, and all were anxious to see how bad or stupid their neighbors were.

"I will send my honest old Minister to the weavers," thought the Emperor. "He can judge best how the stuff looks, for he is intelligent, and nobody understands his office better than he."

So the good old Minister went into the room where the two swindlers sat working at the empty looms.

"Heaven preserve us!" he thought, and opened his eyes wide. "I cannot see anything at all," but he did not say so. Both swindlers bade him be so good as to come near, and asked him if he did not admire the exquisite pattern and the beautiful colors. They pointed to the empty looms, and the poor old Minister opened his eyes wider, but he could see nothing, for there was nothing to be seen.

"Good Lord!" he thought, "can I be so stupid? I should never have thought so, and nobody must know it! Is it possible that I am not fit for my office? No, no, I cannot say that I was unable to see the cloth."

"Well, have you got nothing to say?" said one, as he wove.

"Oh, it is very pretty, quite enchanting!" said the old Minister, peering through his spectacles. "What a pattern, and what colors! I shall tell the Emperor that I am very much pleased with it."

"Well, we are glad of that," said both weavers, and they named the colors to him and explained the curious pattern. The old Minister listened attentively, that he might relate to the Emperor what they said; and he did so.

Now, the swindlers asked for more money, more silk and gold, which they required for weaving. They kept it all for themselves, and not a thread came near the loom, but they continued, as hitherto, to work at the empty looms.

Soon afterwards the Emperor sent another honest courtier to the weavers to see how they were getting on, and if the cloth was nearly finished. Like the old Minister, he looked and looked, but could see nothing, as there was nothing to be seen.

"Is it not a beautiful piece of cloth?" said the two swindlers, showing and explaining the magnificent pattern, which, however, was not there at all.

"I am not stupid," thought the man. "Is it therefore my good appointment for which I am not fit? It is ludicrous, but I must not let anyone know it" and he praised the cloth, which he did not see, and expressed his pleasure at the beautiful colors and the fine pattern. "Yes, it is quite enchanting," he said to the Emperor.

Everybody in the whole town was talking about the splendid cloth. At last the Emperor wished to see it while it was still on the loom. With a whole company of chosen men, including two honest councilors who had already been there, he went to the two clever swindlers, who were now weaving as hard as they could, but without using any thread.

"Is it not *magnifique?*" said both the honest statesmen. "Will your Majesty see what a pattern and what colors?" And they pointed to the empty looms, for they imagined the others could see the cloth.

"What is this?" thought the Emperor. "I do not see anything at all. This is terrible! Am I stupid? Am I unfit to be emperor? That would indeed be the most dreadful thing that could happen to me."

"Yes, it is very fine," said the Emperor. "It has our highest approval!"; and nodding contentedly, he gazed at the empty loom, for he did not like to say that he could see nothing. All his attendants who were with him looked and looked, and although they could not see anything more than the others, they said, like the Emperor. "It is very fine." And all advised him to wear the new magnificent clothes at a great procession that was soon to take place.

"It is *magnifique*! Beautiful, excellent!" went from mouth to mouth, and everybody seemed to be delighted. The Emperor gave each of the swindlers the cross of the order of knighthood and the title of Imperial Court Weavers.

All through the night before the procession was due to take place, the swindlers were up, and had more than sixteen candles burning. People could see that they were busy getting the Emperor's new clothes ready. They pretended to take the cloth from the loom, they snipped the air with big scissors, they sewed needles without thread, and said at last, "Now the Emperor's new clothes are ready!"

The Emperor, with all his noblest courtiers, then came in; and both the swindlers held up one arm as if they held something, and said, "See, here are the trousers! Here is the coat! Here is the cloak! and so on. They are all as light as a cobweb! They make one feel as if one had nothing on at all, but that is just the beauty of it."

"Yes!" said all the courtiers; but they could not see anything, for there was nothing to be seen.

"Will it please your Majesty graciously to take off your clothes?" said the swindlers. "Then we may help your Majesty into the new clothes before the large looking-glass!"

The Emperor took off all his clothes, and the swindlers pretended to put the new clothes upon him, one piece after another; and the Emperor looked at himself in the glass from every side.

"Oh, how well they look! How well they fit!" said all. "What a pattern! What colors! That is a splendid dress!"

"They are waiting outside with the canopy which is to be borne over your Majesty in the procession," said the chief master of the ceremonies.

"Yes, I am quite ready," said the Emperor. "Does not my suit fit me quite marvelously?" And he turned once more to the looking-glass, that people should think he admired his garments.

The chamberlains, who were to carry the train, fumbled with their hands on the ground, as if they were lifting up a train. Then they pretended to hold something up in their hands; they dared not let people know that they could not see anything.

And so the Emperor marched in the procession under the beautiful canopy, and all who saw him in the street and out of the windows exclaimed, "How marvelous the Emperor's new suit is! What a long train he has! How well it fits him!" Nobody would let others know that he saw nothing, for then he would have been unfit for his office or too stupid. None of the Emperor's clothes had ever been such a success.

"But he has nothing on at all," said a little child. "Good heavens! Hear what the little innocent says!" said the father, and then each whispered to the other what the child said. "He has nothing on, a little child says he has nothing on at all!"

"He has nothing on at all!" "He has nothing on at all!" cried all the people at last. And the Emperor too was feeling very worried, for it seemed to him that they were right, but he thought to himself, "All the same I must keep the procession going now." And he held himself stiffer than ever, and the chamberlains walked on and held up the train that was not there at all.

# *Henny-penny*

(England)

One day Henny-penny was picking up corn in the corn yard when—whack!—something hit her upon the head.

"Goodness gracious me!" said Henny-penny. "I believe the sky's a-going to fall! I must go and tell the king."

So she went along and she went along and she went along till she met Cocky-locky. "Where are you going, Henny-penny?" says Cocky-locky.

"Oh! I'm going to tell the king the sky's a-falling," says Henny-penny.

"May I come with you?" says Cocky-locky.

"Certainly," says Henny-penny. So Henny-penny and Cocky-locky went to tell the king the sky was falling.

They went along, and they went along, and they went along, till they met Ducky-daddles. "Where are you going to, Henny-penny and Cocky-locky?" says Ducky-daddles.

"Oh! We're going to tell the king the sky's a-falling," said Henny-penny and Cocky-locky.

"May I come with you?" says Ducky-daddles.

"Certainly," said Henny-penny and Cocky-locky. So Henny-penny, Cocky-locky, and Ducky-daddles went to tell the king the sky was a-falling.

So they went along, and they went along, and they went along, till they met Goosey-poosey. "Where are you going to, Henny-penny, Cocky-locky, and Ducky-daddles?" said Goosey-poosey.

"Oh! We're going to tell the king the sky's a-falling," said Henny-penny and Cocky-locky and Ducky-daddles.

"May I come with you?" said Goosey-poosey.

"Certainly," said Henny-penny, Cocky-locky, and Ducky-daddles. So Henny-penny, Cocky-locky, Ducky-daddles, and Goosey-poosey went to tell the king the sky was a-falling.

So they went along, and they went along, and they went along, till they met Turkey-lurkey. "Where are you going, Henny-penny, Cocky-locky, Ducky-daddles, and Goosey-poosey?" says Turkey-lurkey.

"Oh! We're going to tell the king the sky's a-falling," said Henny-penny, Cocky-locky, Ducky-daddles, and Goosey-poosey.

"May I come with you? Henny-penny, Cocky-locky, Ducky-daddles, and Goosey-poosey?" said Turkey-lurkey.

"Why certainly Turkey-lurkey," said Henny-penny, Cocky-locky, Ducky-daddles, and Goosey-poosey. So Henny-penny, Cocky-locky, Ducky-daddles, Goosey-poosey, and Turkey-lurkey all went to tell the king the sky was a-falling.

So they went along, and they went along, and they went along, till they met Foxy-woxy, and Foxy-woxy said to Henny-penny, Cocky-locky, Ducky-daddles, Goosey-poosey, and Turkey-lurkey, "Where are you going, Henny-penny, Cocky-locky, Ducky-daddles, Goosey-poosey, and Turkey-lurkey?"

And Henny-penny, Cocky-locky, Ducky-daddles, Goosey-poosey, and Turkey-lurkey said to Foxy-woxy, "We're going to tell the king the sky's a-falling."

"Oh! But this is not the way to the king, Henny-penny, Cocky-locky, Ducky-daddles, Goosey-poosey, and Turkey-lurkey," says Foxy-woxy. "I know the proper way. Shall I show it to you?"

"Why certainly, Foxy-woxy," said Henny-penny, Cocky-locky, Ducky-daddles, Goosey-poosey, and Turkey-lurkey. So Henny-penny, Cocky-locky, Ducky-daddles, Goosey-poosey, Turkey-lurkey, and Foxy-woxy all went to tell the king the sky was a-falling. So they went along, and they went along, and they went along, till they came to a narrow and dark hole.

Now this was the door of Foxy-woxy's cave. But Foxy-woxy said to Henny-penny, Cocky-locky, Ducky-daddles, Goosey-poosey, and Turkey-lurkey, "This is the short way to the king's palace. You'll soon get there if you follow me. I will go first and you come after, Henny-penny, Cocky-locky, Ducky daddles, Goosey-poosey, and Turkey-lurkey."

"Why of course, certainly, without doubt, why not?" said Henny-penny, Cocky-locky, Ducky-daddles, Goosey-poosey, and Turkey-lurkey.

So Foxy-woxy went into his cave, and he didn't go very far but turned round to wait for Henny-penny, Cocky-locky, Ducky-daddles,

Goosey-poosey, and Turkey-lurkey. So at last, first Turkey-lurkey went through the dark hole into the cave. He hadn't gotten far when "Hrumph," Foxy-woxy snapped off Turkey-lurkey's head and threw his body over his left shoulder. Then Goosey-poosey went in, and "Hrumph," off went her head and Goosey-poosey was thrown beside Turkey-lurkey. Then Ducky-daddles waddled down, and "Hrumph," snapped Foxy-woxy, and Ducky-daddles' head was off and Ducky-daddles was thrown alongside Turkey-lurkey and Goosey-poosey. Then Cocky-locky strutted down into the cave and he hadn't gone far when, "Snap! Hrumph!" went Foxy-woxy and Cocky-locky was thrown alongside Turkey-lurkey, Goosey-poosey, and Ducky-daddles.

But Foxy-woxy had made two bites at Cocky-locky, and when the first snap only hurt Cocky-locky, but didn't kill him, he called out to Henny-penny. So she turned tail and ran back home, so she never told the king the sky was a-falling.

# *Wit or Noodle*

(China)

Can we ever know and understand other people? Do we sometimes misjudge others? Well, let me tell you about the son of a very rich man who lived a long time ago in China. This man had only one son and he tried to buy the best scholars to tutor him because his son seemed to be stupid in word and deed. Other youngsters jeered him and called him The Dull One.

Everything this son did seemed to end in catastrophe. For instance when he would serve a bowl of sweet and sour soup to one of his father's guests, invariably some of it ended up on the front of the guest. When he brought tea everyone in close proximity ducked and made sure they protected their body parts from hot splashes.

If someone asked him the easiest question, the son just scratched his head, shifted from one foot to another and said "hmmmm, then ahhhhh, and ummmm." His answers were always jumbled and listeners laughed at him and called him Dull Noodle. No one could take him seriously.

As was the custom at that time, fathers arranged marriages for their sons with the daughters of important families in the same region. Dull Noodle's father arranged a marriage for his son while he was still young and could pass for being clever.

Dull Noodle's future father-in-law regretted the pact he had agreed to when it became apparent that his daughter's future husband might not be the best, smartest choice. When Dull Noodle's

:her recognized the cooling relationship, he gave his son one hundred pieces of silver.

"My son, you need to go out into the world and learn and show your future bride that you are worthy." Silently the father thought to himself, "the blind beggar at my gate has more quickness and wit than my son. He must have learned things from being out in the streets and spending time with others."

Dull Noodle left home and wandered about looking for someone to teach him and help him win his bride. On his third day out seeking learning, he came to a lovely garden. In this garden was a small pool. The gardener stood there shaking his head mournfully, saying,

*"Here's water sparkling to the brim,*
*all it needs are fishes in it to swim!"*

Dull Noodle found this little verse enchanting. He offered to pay twenty silver pieces if the man would teach it to him. Of course the gardener was pleased and decided to add more bits of wisdom, such as "A fool and his money are soon at some distance from each other."

"I want only bits of wisdom," Dull Noodle told the gardener. After they worked on it for a while, he could say the rhyme by heart. He gratefully paid the gardener and went on his way.

At the next village, Dull Noodle found an old farmer with a cart stopped at the edge of a deep stream that had only a single board across it. As the farmer looked for another board to help him get across the stream, he tugged at his wiry beard and muttered,

*"One puny plank will not suffice,*
*on which to move a load of rice."*

Dull Noodle liked the sound of this little rhyme and rushed up to the farmer and asked him to teach it to him for twenty pieces of silver. Of course the old man was more than willing and thought of many ways he could spend this money. He and Dull Noodle sat down on a fallen log and it didn't take too long for the pupil to repeat it easily. The farmer was so pleased that he offered to teach him, "A fool and his money are soon strangers to each other," but Dull Noodle wasn't interested. The silver exchanged hands and Dull Noodle continued on his travel repeating what he had learned to make sure he wouldn't forget them.

He traveled until he came to the woods and there he found two hunters. They were aiming their weapons at a brightly colored bird as it flitted back and forth between two huts. They were chanting, "From east to west the red bird flies, now which man wins, and which one sighs?"

This captured the attention of Dull Noodle and it was easy to ask the hunters to teach him this for twenty silver coins apiece. The hunters were pleased and offered to additionally teach him, "A fool's pocket leaks money," but Dull Noodle thanked them and refused their kind offer.

Since he had spent almost all of his coins, Dull Noodle turned homeward. As he entered the city gate, he saw a guest taking leave of his host and overheard his parting words,

*"I've much to say, but time is short,*
*I'll tell the rest to you at court."*

Dull Noodle needed to learn this too so he caught up with the parting guest and asked him if he would please repeat his verse. When the man saw the coins held out to him, he quickly did so. "I'll give you one more thought, if you want. A fool's money runs away faster than a burbling stream," but Dull Noodle declined his offer. He gave the last of his money to the departing guest and hurried on, pleased that he had spent his pieces of silver so wisely and well.

He went directly to his future bride's home and was surprised to find it brightly lit with festive lanterns.

"I wonder how my future bride's family knew I would be returning today for our wedding?" There was a flurry of attention caused by his arrival. "Well, that is quite befitting the arrival of the happy bridegroom," he thought. He graciously was escorted to a place by the feast.

The ushers, surprised and outraged by Dull Noodle's presence, decided they might have some fun at his expense. The ushers realized that Dull Noodle had no idea that his intended bride was about to be married to another. When they brought soup to the other guests, they gave Dull Noodle just warm water in his bowl and watched his face when he tasted it.

Bowl in hand, Dull Noodle was about to drink when he appeared to get an idea and said, "Here's water sparkling to the brim, how sad no fishes in it swim!"

The surprised ushers quickly exchanged the water for soup. When the main course was served however, they couldn't resist giving Dull Noodle one chopstick instead of a pair. This didn't bother Dull Noodle in the least and he said in a friendly manner,

*"One puny plank will not suffice,*
*on which to move a load of rice."*

of the guests were amazed at Dull Noodle's clever approach to such an embarrassing social situation. The ushers, in their turn were shamefaced and bright red of face as they brought him a pair of chopsticks.

The bride in her red wedding dress stood with the groom, ready to be married and heard Dull Noodle's remark,

*"From east to west the red bird flies,*
*now which man wins, and which one sighs?"*

The wedding guests began to admire this man who could coolly compose verses while watching the celebration of his intended bride's marriage with another groom. Obviously Dull Noodle was not nearly as foolish as they had thought. Perhaps the girl's proud father was wrong in not honoring his agreement.

Dull Noodle was beginning to feel bored with everything that was going on and besides he was tired from his travels. He wanted to leave but he still had one of his verses left. He found the bride's father and covered a yawn and recited the last bit he had learned,

*"I've much to say, but time is short,*
*I'll tell the rest to you at court."*

The bride's father recognized the threat of a lawsuit for not living up to his first marriage contract. He became quite frightened, went to the other suitor and led him out of the house. Quickly he then led Dull Noodle to his daughter's side and the wedding was as many people remarked, a very lovely one.

People stopped referring to the new bridegroom with the former insulting name and instead showed him respect due to a man who could solely through his wit, marry into the most important family in the district. Of course, the new bridegroom's new family never showed anything but delight in having such a bright son-in-law in their midst. They felt he refrained from anger and thereby showed his wisdom. They were reminded of the proverb, "If you are patient in one moment of anger, you will escape a hundred days of sorrow."

# *Juan Bobo*

(Puerto Rico)

In a small village, there lived a mother and her two children. Pedro, her oldest son was considered the smart one; his brother Juan, used to do so many ridiculous things that everyone called him "Juan Bobo."

This poor little family cut sugarcane in the field during the day to earn a living. It was a relief when they left the fields went home in the late afternoons.

One day, the mother left the fields early to go home and prepare supper. Pedro and Juan were going home slowly because they were burdened down with firewood.

"I am going to climb a mango tree and pick some mangos because I am so hungry," Juan Bobo told his brother as they passed a grove of mango trees.

"Juan Bobo! Don't be foolish! The owner will cut your hands off if he sees you stealing his mangos!" warned Pedro.

Juan Bobo told him, "I just need some of the luscious mango fruit. I must have some," and he went to pick the mangos. He ate a few of them and then ran after his brother, "Pedro, I did not see the owner anywhere near the trees."

After that, Juan Bobo continued to pick mangos every night on his way home from the sugarcane fields. However, the owner wasn't as dumb as Juan thought he was. He noticed that someone was stealing his mangos. "I want to catch that mango thief!" declared the owner. "I know what I can do to catch him. I will make a doll out of old clothes and filled with tar." He proceeded to do that and placed the doll among the mango trees.

The very next day, as usual Juan Bobo went to the mango trees to steal some fruit as usual. Pedro was still worried and warned Juan, "Sooner or later you will be caught by the owner."

By this time Juan wasn't worried, "The mangos do not belong to anyone since I have never seen anyone among the trees." As luck would have it, that very day Juan Bobo saw somebody but figured it was only someone else trying to steal mangos too. Juan called out to the one he saw in a loud voice, "Ho there. Who are you?"

The person, who was really the tar scarecrow, of course did not answer Juan. It just sat there. Juan got very close and crept up on the doll because he thought someone was trying to hide from him. Juan got very close and then swiftly gave the man a kick from behind. "OOOFF," exploded Juan when his foot got stuck in the tar doll.

Juan Bobo thought the man was trying to hold him. "I know what you want!" roared Juan. "You want all of the mangos for yourself." With that, Juan tried to slap the man with his hand.

"Blah!" moaned Juan. "Now I know what you are up to. You want to fight!"

With that, Juan butted his head into the man so that he could free himself, but horrors! His head stuck into the tar scarecrow. When Juan saw that the man wouldn't let him go he began yelling, "Help! This great hulk is trying to kill me! I am almost dead."

The owner of the garden and grove of mango trees heard Juan's cry for help.

"Ha!" he remarked in a very happy voice. "I have finally caught the thief red-handed." The owner didn't hurry to let Juan get free because he wanted to make sure he suffered a little bit longer. The owner took his time finishing his supper and then walked quietly to the mango trees.

There was Juan Bobo. Now he was crying and very tired from the struggle to free himself. The owner snatched up a tree branch and beat Juan Bobo. As if that wasn't bad enough, when Juan got home he received another beating from his mother and yet another from his brother who had told him not to steal mangos. The final indignity for Juan was that he was sent to bed hungry—without supper!

# *Coyote and the Lizards*

(Navajo)

Coyote was happiest when he was spying on someone or poking his nose into their business. It was just that kind of a day. He was looking for somebody to spy on when he came upon a group of lizards on top of a big, flat rock with one sloping side. They were playing a game that was strange to him. They were taking turns sliding down the steep slope on small flat rocks. He decided to learn all about it, so he joined them.

He saw that each time, the slider picked up his rock at the bottom of the slope and carried it up the hill on his back. Coyote trotted over to the rock and sat down. The lizards went on with their play and pretended they didn't see him.

Now Coyote didn't like to be ignored, the least the lizards could do was to notice him. He scooted over a little closer and began to talk to the lizards. "That looks like fun! What do you call this game?" he asked.

One of the lizards answered, "We just call it sliding," without even looking at him.

"It looks interesting. I'd like to join you in your sliding game," said Coyote as he scooted a little closer to them.

With this, all of the lizards turned and looked at him coldly through their lizard eyes. "Go play your own games. We are lizards and this is our game. You aren't a lizard and you don't know how to play our game."

Coyote wheedled, "But I can learn. Really your game looks like a very simple one. I can just stand on the rock and slide down too. Come on, let me try, I'll show you I can do it."

An old wrinkled lizard hissed. "This game is not as simple as you think. It is very dangerous and you could get killed. Maybe the first time you do it everything would be all right but the second time when you ride down the big rock you'd be smashed flat, flat, flat, flat!"

Coyote was offended. None of the lizards had been smashed. Why should he? He didn't believe a word of what the old lizard said. He whined and wheedled for them to let him try it. He would show them.

The wrinkled old lizard got tired of his whimpering so he said, "Well, just once cousin. You can ride the small flat rock but do not ask to ride the big one."

Really! thought Coyote. He intended to ride the big one too but he kept quiet for now. He slid down the little one just to show them how well he could do it. After that it would be easy to persuade them to let him try the big one.

Several of the lizards placed the small flat rock in position for Coyote. They looked at him with puckered faces. "I don't know why you want to play our games. I know you play games chasing rabbits and kangaroo rats and all sorts of other creatures. Running games are more to your taste and talent. You are such a fast runner why don't you play your own games?"

Arrogantly Coyote stepped on the flat rock. It tilted down the runway and with a scraping sound he flashed down the hill and before he reached the bottom of the slide, he jumped off. He picked up the rock and trotted back up the hill. "See," he panted, "I can do it. Let me use the big rock now!"

"We warned you. We don't want you to try the big rock. However, if you want to risk your life, it is your own problem when you get smashed flat, flat, flat, flat!" said the old lizard looking at him with a stern lizard look. "Get the big rock for him," the old lizard told the young lizards. They waddled away silently and came back with it. They placed the big rock on the very edge of the runway and then they slithered away.

Coyote was not at all afraid. He ran out to the rock, tipped it a little and once again he was sliding down the runway with his tail flying behind him. The big rock caught on a smaller rock half way down the slide and flipped into the air. Coyote was frightened half out of his skin. His ears were flapping and his paws and claws were digging into the air. This wasn't nearly as much fun as the first ride he thought as he flipped through the air. He hit the ground and rolled over in the dust. He saw the big rock right behind him coming down on top of him.

"Maybe I should have listened," he thought. "I am really going to be smashed flat, flat, flat, flat, just like old lizard told me." The big rock crashed into him and did indeed smash Coyote. The lizards were on top of the slide looking down at him.

"Even though he was no friend of mine, it still makes me sad to see poor foolish Coyote smashed so flat," observed the old lizard.

"The worst part is that he is right in the middle of our runway," announced one of the young lizards. "It wouldn't be right to leave him there but he is so heavy—how are we going to move him?"

"It would be simpler to bring him back to life," wheezed a third lizard. "Then he could leave without us having to move him."

The oldest lizard stroked his scales and said, "You have a very good idea young one. Let's do it."

They slid down to Coyote in a single file and made a tight circle around him so they could work their spell in private. Using their old lizard secrets they brought him back to life. "Now go along with you Coyote," the old lizard ordered him. "After this, don't try to play lizard games. We don't want to have to go through this again."

Coyote was glad to be alive again. He got up, dusted himself off and dashed for home as fast as his four sore legs could go.

# *Rabbit and the Otter*

(Cherokee)

One sunny day, Rabbit and Otter were talking and bragging about who could do what the best. Rabbit boasted, "Look over there on the lake, Otter. See that duck swimming out in the middle? I can catch it easier than you can. Do you want to bet?"

Otter looked out to the lake where the duck was gliding along enjoying the day. "No problem there," said the Otter. "Of course I can easily do that and beat you."

With that, Rabbit dove into the water and threw a noose over the neck of the duck. The very next thing, before the blink of an eye, the duck took off and flew away with Rabbit hanging on to the rope.

Rabbit yelled, "Stop it duck. I don't like this flying." No longer was Rabbit boasting as he saw the duck starting to fly higher and faster. Eventually, since the duck wasn't following his orders, frantic Rabbit lets go of the rope and fell to the earth landing in a hollow tree stump with a thump. Now Rabbit was in a real predicament. He was tightly trapped inside the stump and after quite some time, hunger set in.

After a long time of being hungry, Rabbit ate his fur. Time passed and he heard some children begging their father. "Father, cut a hole in this stump for us. It will be the perfect one we need for what we plan to do."

The father questioned his children to make sure they really wanted him to cut a hole in the stump and then he took his axe and did just that. As the father struck the first "whomp" onto the stump, Rabbit quickly escaped. Not only had he lost his bet with Otter, but there he now stood in total humiliation because of his ragged appearance and now absent tail.

And that is why Rabbit no longer has a long tail that he can swish around. Instead, his tail is just a puff of fur.

# *Manka the Clever*

(Czechoslovakia)

Long, long ago, there was a rich farmer who was as grasping and unscrupulous as he was rich. Somehow, he always got the better of his poor neighbors and when negotiating bargains, he always drove a hard bargain.

One of his neighbors was a humble shepherd. He had worked for the rich farmer and had been promised a heifer for his labor. When the work was done and it was time for the shepherd to be paid, the farmer refused to give the shepherd the heifer. The shepherd had no choice but to take the matter before the local magistrate.

The magistrate was an insecure young man who did not have much experience, but he did have a fake look of confidence about him. He carefully listened to both sides. First he heard the shepherd and then the rich farmer. After some careful thought and much stroking of his chin, he declared that, "Instead of deciding this case, I will put a riddle to both of you. The one of you that makes the best answer will receive the heifer. Do you agree to this?"

The farmer and the shepherd both nodded their heads and agreed to this proposal.

The magistrate then said, "Well then, here is my riddle. What is the swiftest thing in the world? What is the sweetest thing? What is the richest? Carefully think out your answers and tomorrow at this same time, meet here again."

The farmer stomped out of the magistrate's office and kicked up dust as he went on down the road to home.

"What kind of a magistrate is this? Of course, he didn't know that if he had let me keep the heifer, I would have sent him a bushel of pears as my thanks. Now, I'm possibly going to lose the heifer since I can't think of any answer to his foolish riddle."

When he arrived home, the farmer's wife recognized his ill temper and asked, "What is the matter husband?"

"Ah wife," he responded, "it is the new young magistrate. The old magistrate would have certainly given me the heifer with no argument, but this young fellow is new. He thinks he will decide the case by giving us riddles. Imagine! Riddles!"

"What riddle did he give you husband?" she asked.

He asked us, "What is the swiftest thing in the world? What is the sweetest thing? What is the richest? That is what he gave us for riddles."

His wife clapped her hands and smiled, "That is not a problem. I know the answer to that obvious riddle. Our gray mare is the swiftest thing in the world. You know yourself that nothing ever passes us on the road. As for the sweetest, did you ever taste honey any sweeter than ours? Our bees use nothing but the sweetest pollens. And of course, there is nothing that could be richer than our chest of golden ducats. They have been collecting for over forty years now."

Her husband gave her a big smile. "Good wife, you are right. You are certainly right! No problem, the heifer will remain ours with your wise answers."

When the shepherd got home to his spare cottage, he was depressed and sad. The first one to greet him when he entered his home was his daughter Manka. He liked to call her his clever Manka.

"Dear father. You look so downcast. What did the magistrate decide?"

With a big sigh, the shepherd told her, "I am afraid that I have lost the heifer. The magistrate listened to our case after stroking his chin a time or two, and he gave us a riddle. Tomorrow we must give him our answers and then he will make the decision on the heifer."

Clever Manka sat her father down at the kitchen table and gave him a cup of cool water to drink. "Perhaps I can be of some help. What riddle did he give you?"

"Well dear daughter, it is one I cannot solve. What is the swiftest thing in the world? What is the sweetest thing? What is the richest thing? I have no answers for this."

They spent a quiet evening before the fire together. The next day as the shepherd was ready to leave for the magistrate's, Manka gave him some answers to the riddle. Truly, Manka was clever. When the shepherd reached the magistrate's place the farmer stood there rubbing his hands together with glee and self-importance.

The magistrate greeted the two men and then repeated his riddle. The farmer answered first. He stood proud and cleared his throat with a pompous attitude and gave his answer. "The swiftest thing in the world is my gray mare of course. Why do I say that? Because no other horse ever passes us on the road. The sweetest? That is also easy. The honey from my beehives is surely the sweetest in the world. And as for the richest? What could possibly be richer than my chest full of golden ducats?"

The farmer looked triumphant and turned to the magistrate with confidence and boldness. The magistrate just looked at him coolly and then turned to the shepherd. "What answers do you have for the riddle?"

The shepherd bowed politely and in a soft voice he answered. "The swiftest thing in the world is thought. Thought can run any distance in the mere twinkling of an eye. The sweetest thing of all is sleep, for when a man is tired from working and sad from life's problems, what could be sweeter? As for the richest thing it must be the earth itself since out of the earth comes all of the riches of the world."

The magistrate glowed at the shepherd. "Good! Now that I have heard your answers to my riddle, the shepherd obviously earned the heifer."

As the magistrate shook the shepherd's hand in congratulations he asked, "Tell me. Where did you get these answers? Somehow I have the feeling that they did not come from out of your own head?"

The shepherd looked embarrassed and then gave the magistrate his truthful answer. "I confess that my clever daughter Manka gave me the answers."

Again, stroking his chin in thought, the magistrate decided to give the shepherd another test. "To test your daughter's cleverness, I have another task." He then sent his clerk for ten eggs. As he gave them to the shepherd he directed him, "Take these eggs to Manka and tell her to have them hatched out by tomorrow and to bring me the chicks."

The shepherd carefully carried the eggs home. Manka opened the cottage door curious as to what had happened. "The magistrate gave you another task after I confessed that you had given me the answer to the riddle."

Manka laughed at the earnest look on her father's face. "Tell me what this task is?"

Her father handed her the ten eggs and relayed the magistrate's message. Manka laughed when she heard this. "Take a handful of millet father and go right back to the magistrate. Tell him that I send him this millet. If he plants it, grows it, and has it harvested by tomorrow, I will bring him the ten chicks and he can feed them the ripe grain!"

The shepherd took the millet, and with a smile on his face, he returned to the magistrate's. After he told the magistrate what Manka said, and gave him the millet, the magistrate doubled over with laughter.

"Your daughter is indeed clever," he told the shepherd. "If she is as beautiful as she is clever, I think I would like to marry her. Tell her to come see me, but she must come neither by day nor by night, neither riding nor walking, neither dressed nor undressed."

"Woe is me." mumbled the shepherd to himself as he returned home. He told Manka what the magistrate had said. She waited until the next dawn when night was gone and day had not yet quite arrived. She wrapped herself in a fishnet and threw one leg over a goat's back and kept one foot on the ground. She then traveled to the magistrate's house.

Now, I ask you—did she go dressed? No, she wasn't dressed since a fishnet is not clothing. Did she go undressed? Of course not, for wasn't she covered with the fishnet? Did she walk to the magistrate's? No she didn't walk for she went with one leg thrown over a goat. But, did she ride? Of course she didn't ride for wasn't she walking on one foot!

"Here I am Mr. Magistrate. I have come neither by day nor by night, neither riding nor walking, neither dressed nor undressed."

This delighted the young magistrate. "You are surely clever Manka. I am so pleased by you, your mind, and your looks that I have another question for you. Will you marry me?"

Manka blushed and said, "Yes."

They were married shortly thereafter. "There is one thing my dear Manka," the magistrate said. "You are not to use that cleverness of yours at my expense. I won't have you interfering in any of my decisions. In fact, if you ever give advice to anyone who comes to me for judgment, I'll send you out of my home at once and send you on your way back to your father."

All went well for quite some time. They made a happy couple. Manka busied herself in making their home a warm and happy one. She was careful not to interfere with the work of the magistrate.

Then one day, two farmers came to the magistrate to have him settle a dispute. One of the farmers told the magistrate, "I have a mare which has foaled in the marketplace. The colt ran under the wagon of another farmer there and the owner of the wagon immediately claimed the colt to be his."

The magistrate had not been entirely concentrating on what the farmer told him and said carelessly, "The man who found the colt under his wagon is of course the owner of the colt."

The owner of the mare was shaking his head as he left the magistrate's house. On his way out he met Manka and stopped to tell her what had happened. Manka was ashamed of her husband for making such a foolish decision. She told the farmer, "Come back this afternoon with a fishing net and stretch it across the dusty road. When the magistrate sees you he will become curious and will come out and ask you what you are doing. Answer him that you are just catching fish. I am sure that he will then ask you how you can expect to catch fish in a dusty road. You only have to tell him it is just as easy for you to catch fish in a dusty road as it is for a wagon to foal. Being a bright man, he will see the injustice of his decision and have the colt returned to you. There is only one thing I ask you. Remember that you must not let him find out that it was I who told you to do this. That is important."

That afternoon, the magistrate was sitting at a table beside a window and he looked out. He saw a man stretching a fishnet across the dusty road in front of him. Being curious, the magistrate went out and asked the man, "What on earth are you doing?"

The answer he got was, "I am fishing!"

"Are you daft? How can you be fishing in this dusty road?" the magistrate asked him.

In a very respectful voice, the man answered, "Well, it is just as easy for me to catch fish in a dusty road as it is for a wagon to foal."

When he heard this, the magistrate recognized the man from the case in the morning as the owner of the mare.

"I am forced to confess that what you have said is true. Of course the colt belongs to your mare and must be returned to you." The magistrate stroked his chin in thoughtfulness, "Who put you up to this? Tell me. You did not think of it yourself did you?"

The farmer tried his best not to tell the magistrate the truth, but the magistrate persisted in his questioning until he found out that Manka was at the bottom of it. The magistrate became quite angry and went into his house and called, "Manka! Manka, come here at once!"

When she stood before him, he looked sad. "Manka," he said. "Did you forget what I told you would happen if you interfered in any of my decisions? You must go home to your father immediately. Don't bother me with any excuses. The matter is settled. I will allow you to take with you the one thing you like best in my house because I won't have people saying that I treated you in a mean way."

Manka stood there and looked at her husband. "Very well, my dear husband. I shall do as you say. I will go home to my father's cottage and take with me the one thing I like best in your house. All I ask is that you please don't make me go until after supper. We have been very happy together and I would appreciate the opportunity to eat one last meal with you. Let us be kind to each other and not have any more harsh words.

I would like us to continue to be kind to each other and then part as friends."

The magistrate sniffled a bit as he agreed to this for he cared deeply for Manka. She prepared a fine supper, which included all of the dishes that were his particular favorites. The magistrate opened a bottle of his very best wine and toasted Manka's health. The supper was so good that the magistrate just ate and ate. The more he ate, the more he drank until he grew drowsy and fell sound asleep in his chair with his head resting in his arms on the table.

Manka quietly had the magistrate carried out to the wagon that was waiting outside to take her back to her father's cottage. The next morning the magistrate awoke in the shepherd's cottage. He opened his eyes wide. "What does this mean?" he roared.

Manka stood beside the bed he was in and said, "Nothing, dear husband, nothing! Remember you told me I might take with me the one thing I liked the very best in your house. Obviously I took you! That is all there is to it."

The magistrate sat up in the bed and rubbed his eyes with his clenched fists. He was amazed. And then, he laughed out loud and full of joy with how Manka had outwitted him. "Manka," he laughed, "you are too clever for me. You win. Come on my love, let us go home."

So together they climbed into the wagon and waved farewell to Manka's father who stood in the doorway. They drove home. The magistrate never again scolded Manka, but whenever there was a difficult decision to be made thereafter, he always said, "I think that we must consult Manka. My wife is a very clever and wise woman."

# *The Honest Shepherd*

(Scotland)

You know how farmers are when they get together. They share their joys and especially their sorrows with each other. Two farmers, who were neighbors, had been at a sale and on their way home they discussed the problems with farming. They had to fertilize their land because with farming demands, the land was almost dead. They agreed, rents were so high, workmen who worked on their farms had to be paid so much, especially if they had skills like carpenters and smiths, that there wasn't much left over for themselves.

One of the farmers called Fergus, said, "All that is true enough, but I think that when they are good workers, what they are paid is no loss. I have good helpers myself, but if they were all like my shepherd Angus, I could go to Spain all winter long. I never saw such a dedicated person, and so truthful beside. He has never once told a lie."

His friend snorted. "I thought you had sense, but a man who never told a lie! Who are you trying to fool? I have never heard of such a man! No man like that exists," he said.

"Well, Angus is an honest man anyway," insisted Fergus.

His friend said, "Hunh! That's only because he has had no reason to tell a lie, I am sure. That's why. No one tells a lie when the truth will do."

"Well," claimed Fergus, "I'll bet you anything he won't tell a lie."

"Ha! I'll bet you twenty pounds he will tell you a lie in front of me within a day," roared his friend.

"Well, all right," agreed Fergus. "It's on. How are you going to try him?"

"Let's leave him alone. I'll come over one day next week and we will try him to find out if he will tell you the truth."

The friend went home. He had a dairymaid on his farm that he admired and he regularly found a reason to see her. He knew that he could trust her so he said, "Morag, I'd appreciate it if you could do something to help me out."

"Of course, I will if I can," she answered.

"You can," he said. "I have some nice stockings here, knee stockings which I have never worn. I want you to take them to Angus the shepherd. I have a large bet on with his master Fergus. There's a black sheep in his flock, and Fergus has a great notion for it since he thinks it's a terribly lucky beastie to have in his flock. I know that it is the first beastie he will ask Angus about when he gets home. I also know Angus will be willing to give you anything in return for the stockings, but don't accept anything from him but the black sheep. If you get the black sheep from him, I will win the bet and you'll get a nice share of it."

Morag looked at her master demurely, "Oh, I'd be ashamed to go out there by myself."

"Shush now, be quiet. You can make the excuse that you have come to see some of my beasties that are out on the hills there," he told Morag.

So, Morag went off with the stockings, straight for the hill, watching to see if she could see Angus. There he was on top of a knoll. Angus saw Morag and he went down to where she was.

"Och! What in the world has sent you out here?" he asked.

"Oh, I came to look for a cow of my master on the hill that's his calf. I also wanted to see you." Morag blushed as she handed Angus the small package she had. "I have a little present here for you. I haven't had a chance to give it to you in private so I brought it with me. Here it is."

"What is it?" asked Angus.

Morag pushed her heel into the ground and twisted it a bit, "Just some stockings I have made for you." She shyly gave him the stockings.

"Well, well, well!" said Angus. "Now, aren't they lovely. And was it really you who made them, Morag?"

"Yes," said Morag. "Many a night I was working on them late in the evening after the others had gone to sleep, in case they saw me knitting them. I knew that if they had seen me, they'd have been watching to see who would be wearing them afterwards. That's the honest truth Angus. That seems to be their occupation, watching and being curious about me.

"Well now Morag, I didn't know that you liked me as much as that," said a blushing Angus.

"Oh," said Morag turning the toe of her shoe into the ground, "I like you more than you like me, Angus."

"Now that's not a fact Morag," said Angus. "What would you like to have in return?"

"Oh, I didn't expect anything in return. I didn't make them for that Angus. I just wanted to make them for you," said Morag as she gave a big smile to Angus.

"I know that Morag, but you must let me give you something. I want to," insisted Angus.

"Well, what I'd like to have would be no loss to you, if you'd give it to me," answered Morag.

"And what might that be?" asked Angus.

Morag looked him straight in the eyes and said, "The black sheep."

"If it were mine, you'd get it! Even if it were a flock!" Angus told her. "But it's the first beastie himself will ask me about, when I go to the farm. He'll say, 'have you got the black sheep?' He thinks more of it that he does for the whole flock."

"Angus, you can make an excuse, can't you? You know the black sheep won't live forever. It's special because it is the first thing I've ever asked you for," said Morag.

Angus went and gathered the sheep and got hold of the black sheep and gave it to Morag. She put a rope on it and left with it. When she arrived, her master was quite pleased to see her leading the sheep.

"You have done very well, Morag. We'll see now if Angus always tells the truth as his master claimed he does." With that, he went on over to see his neighbor Fergus.

"Greetings, Fergus. Has Angus been in since I saw you last?"

"No, I have had no reason to send for him," was the answer.

"Well, send for him now," instructed the farmer. "Now we'll see if Angus always tells the truth as you say he does. Why don't you tell him you have something you want to see him about."

"How do you plan to test him?" inquired Fergus.

"I only want you to ask him everything you usually do, Fergus and I'll ask the rest," chuckled the farmer.

And so, Fergus sent for Angus, saying he had something he wanted to see him about.

Angus didn't know what to do. "I don't know what business he has to talk to me about today, unless he wants to gather the sheep. What will I do when I get there? He'll ask how the flock is. His first question will be about the black sheep. Oh, I wish I had never seen Morag's present!" wailed Angus.

He went and stuck his crook on a mound, and put his jacket on it. There's the farmer now. "What am I going to tell him? I'll say I have lost the black sheep."

"Here you are, Angus," greeted Fergus.

"Yes," said Angus but he couldn't lift his eyes above the buttons on Fergus' jacket.

"How did you leave the flock?"

"All right."

Then Fergus asked the question, "Have you got the black sheep?"

"No," was the answer.

"Och, so the black sheep's lost?"

"Yes."

"Well, well!" answered Fergus. "I'd sooner lose five others than her!"

"I'd sooner, too," mumbled Angus.

"What do you think came over her and made her take off?" asked Fergus.

"The braxy."

"It didn't used to be very bad out there," pondered Fergus.

"No, it wasn't indeed. I haven't lost many since I went there."

"Well, well! She was a pretty beastie and a lucky beastie in the flock," moaned Fergus.

"Indeed, that she was. A lucky beastie. I didn't lose many since she was out there in the flock."

"Oh, for certain, the beastie you take a notion to will be the first one you'll lose," remarked Fergus.

"Right you are sir. I've always noticed that myself."

"Yes, so have I, Angus. Did you bring the skin home?"

Angus thought to himself, "Here it comes."

"No," he said to himself. "No, nor hide nor hair! It's too difficult! I haven't got it. God help me! What will I do now? That way won't do. I must try another. I'll say it has been stolen, and he'll never ask for the skin!"

"I have walked every inch of the hill. I've looked in every hole and stream. I've been everywhere. I couldn't find her alive or dead, not even a wisp of her wool caught on a bush or fence, sir."

"Aye, aye! She must have been stolen."

"Nothing surer," agreed Angus.

"Well, well! I have never heard the like. You know, it seems as if there are thieves everywhere! Did you miss any others besides her?"

"No, I didn't, sir."

"Well Angus, she can't have gone far."

"Who knows?"

"No, Angus. Look, if it was a thief who meant to sell sheep, he would have taken as many as he could. Surely she can't have gone far at all. Let's send for the police. Even if the meat has been eaten, the wool won't have been."

"Look here! (said Angus to himself) the police will go out, and they'll find Morag has the sheep, and Morag will go to prison. There's only one way to go. I might as well go to prison myself, as to get her in trouble. What shall I do now? Lies won't do any good, only the truth will, be it soft or hard. If it can be paid for, I don't care if he keeps it off my wages. If that can't be done, he can just do what he likes with me."

Angus went off, took his jacket and his crook with him, and went straight to the farmhouse. When he got there, he went straight to the kitchen. Morag's master was waiting for him in the room along with Fergus. The farmer was told that Angus had come. Angus was sent for and he went down to the room. Suddenly it seemed quite hot and Angus was wiping sweat from his brow.

"You have come Angus," said the farmer.

"Yes."

"My goodness, how you are perspiring. How can that be? It is not hot." asked the farmer.

"No, you are right, it is cold right enough."

"How did you leave the flock out there, Angus?" asked the farmer.

"All right. Nothing wrong," was his answer.

"Have you got the black sheep?" asked the farmer, just waiting for Angus to lie.

Angus didn't say a word. He just stood there and hung his head.

"Have you not got the black sheep at all, Angus?"

"No, I have not."

"What happened to her? She was the favorite of Fergus."

"I gave her away."

"Have you sold her?"

"No, sir, I wouldn't sell her."

"Whom did you give her to?"

"I gave her to the dairymaid, Morag. She came out about a week ago with some presents for me, and though I'd have given her my heart, she wouldn't take anything but the black sheep in return. Though, I'm sorry enough today for that. But what good will that do? If I can pay for it I'm willing enough to have it taken out of my wages. If that can't be done, it seems you can do what you like with me."

"Well, well, well and well again Angus. I never heard the like of that! I hear that you have a great notion for that dairymaid. Were you giving her a dowry out of my goods, or what did you have in mind?" asked Fergus.

"I probably was."

"Well, Angus, I have never heard the like of that. I didn't think you would do it," mused Fergus.

He turned to the farmer, "What do you have to say to him now? I've finished with him."

"Well, actually nothing at all. It looks as if you can stand by what you were saying Fergus, all right."

"Well Angus," said Fergus. "Although you gave away the black sheep you will be forgiven since you have stood by telling only the truth as you have always done. Now, if you hadn't done that, you wouldn't be with me another twenty-four hours. But the best thing for you to do is to marry that dairymaid, and then you'll have both her as well as the black sheep. You won't be a shepherd out on the hill any more. Instead, I think that you will be my manager right here."

Angus stopped hanging his head when he heard this. Nothing had ever turned out so well for him as when he had given away the black sheep! And so, on a lovely sunny day, he married Morag and got his new position as Fergus's manager!

# *The Bootless Fiddler*

(Scotland)

*The tragedy of the battle of Culloden between Scotland and England gives us a heritage of historical facts and stories. There are also stories following this battle that may or may not be fact. The following story concerns the retreat of the defeated Highland forces. These warriors left the battlefield strewn with slaughtered bodies and shattered dreams to trudge home to family. They were not only demoralized and defeated but clothed in scraps and rags covering hungry and exhausted bodies. What more could possibly go wrong?*

A band of MacRaes were headed to Kintail by way of Glenmoriston. They hoped to make it as far as Torghoil where they would seek a place to rest for the night. The weather had been cruel in its cold and dampness. The MacRae soldier, who was a fiddler, lagged behind the others since he was worried for his precious instrument and the damage the weather might wreak on it. He stopped to carefully wrap his instrument in his plaid. He did this in a bend of the path that had heavy brush alongside it.

He heard something ahead and quickly hid himself. It was certainly fortunate that he did this for what he heard was one of the English Duke of Cumberland's troopers. "Butcher" Cumberland's men had orders to kill all rebels they could find.

The fiddler hiding in the brushwood saw an enemy Redcoat passing and instinctively the fiddler sprang at him and dispatched him with his sharp dirk. As he watched the body to make sure that he was dead, the fiddler saw the high boots on the dead man.

Then the fiddler reasoned, "This man has no further need for boots now." The other fact that the fiddler didn't recognize was that he coveted those sturdy boots. His own feet were wrapped in muddy rags. He kneeled down to take the boots off. He tugged at them and he pulled. He twisted the boots and legs but nothing happened. They would just not come off.

He grasped his dirk, which he had just wiped in the brush to clean the blood off, and severed the dead British soldier's legs at the knees. The only thing he could do now was to wrap the boots with legs still in them, along with his fiddle in his plaid. He grabbed his bundle and hurried on his way to catch up with the other Highland stragglers.

At Torghoill, the MacRaes had already received food and drink at an inn friendly to the rebels. Everyone had gone to the outbuildings to sleep. Since he had lagged behind, the innkeeper who had served him refreshments stopped him as he headed to the big barn to join the others in plumping up some hay for a soft bed to sleep on.

"No, no," said the man. "They declared that anyone disturbing them before morning would do so at the peril of his life. Don't go there. I will make you a bed in the cow's byre."

The fiddler and the innkeeper went out and into the byre. The fiddler looked around and said, "I'll sleep just fine in front of your brindled cow. The cow's breath will keep me warm."

As soon as he was alone in the byre, the fiddler unwrapped the plaid and took the boots and their legs out. He carefully wiped off and placed his fiddle in the hay. He set about the task of getting the boots separated from the body parts. It took him quite a while to get this job done because he wanted to keep the boots undamaged. At last he got it done, laid down, wrapped himself in his plaid and went to sleep. The moist breath of the cow did indeed warm him.

In the morning, he rose to join his company but first he put his new boots on. They were certainly better than the rags he had used previously on his feet and he rejoiced that they were a perfect fit. He wrapped his fiddle back up carefully in his plaid. Then, he looked at the legs that he had taken from the boots and decided to place them near the head of the still sleeping cow.

The milkmaid came out to the byre later that morning to milk the cow and just stood there screaming and screaming at the very top of her lungs. Everyone in the house rushed out. "The brindled cow has eaten the fiddler and all that is left of him are his two legs!" moaned the innkeeper.

After saying this, the innkeeper got his axe and killed the cow right on the spot. He, with the help of some workers at the inn, buried the cow and the Sassenach's legs in the same grave. Thereafter, when he heard fiddle music being played, or went by the spot where he had buried the cow, he seemed haunted by the memory of the fiddler who was buried inside his brindled cow.

# *Noodleheads*

*It is a profitable thing, if one is wise, to seem foolish.*

Aeschylus

*The humorist does not laugh so much at mankind as he invites mankind to laugh at itself.*

Peter De Vries

# *The Irish Travelers*

(North Carolina, United States)

There were seven Irishmen traveling a while back, and night overtook them. They came to where the road ran alongside of a river. The moon was shining bright, and one of these Irishmen looked over in the water and saw the moon shining down in the middle of the river.

"Look!"

Everyone stopped and came over and looked.

"What in the world is that now?" one of them asked.

"Hit's a yaller cheese," came an idea from one perplexed fellow.

"No," says Pat. He was the biggest one of the seven. "Hit's a lump of gold, and faith-n-b-jabbers we'll get it."

"Now how'll we get it out from there?" the red headed fellow among them asked.

"Faith!" says Pat. "Now I'll tell ye. We'll all climb up in that tree there, see, and we'll all get out on that limb that hangs out just over where the lump of gold is at, see, and then I'll hang down on that limb, see, and then one of you fellers will climb down and take me by the heels, see, and then another'n will climb down over us, see, and take him by the heels, see, and then another'n will climb down and take him by his heels, see, and then we'll all get strung down like that, see, till the last man of all, see, can reach down and take hold on the gold, see, and he'll hand it up, see, and when it gets to me I'll take it down, see, and we'll break it and divide it amongst us all, see, and we'll all be rich forevermore! D'ye see now?"

They all thought that was just fine, and it wasn't long till the seventh man was climbing down to the bottom place. He caught on with one hand and was tryin' to reach for that lump of gold with the other, and Pat's string of men got to swingin' a little. Pat felt his hands about to slip, so he hollers out, "You'uns there below! Hold fast a second while I spit on me hands!"

So Pat let go. And there they were strugglin' and stranglin' and beatin' the water with their hands. Pat he could swim, so he got out quick and reached a pole to 'em and dragged 'em out.

"Oh faith, and now look at what you've done! And one of us poor fellers might have got drownded. Stand there now and let me count yet."

They stood there with the water dreenin' off 'em, and Pat he put his finger on his own chest, says, "Me and myself," then he pointed at the others, says, "and one, two, three, four, five, six! Oh, Oh! Now what'll we do? There's one poor feller's got drownded!"

Well, first one and then another would try to count, but none of 'em thought to count himself in, so they sat there all night lookin' in the water for the one that was drownded, and mournin' and carryin'-on over it till it was daylight.

Then a man came along and saw 'em sittin' there a-cryin' and hoo-hoo-in', and asked what was the matter. So Pat told him how they'd tried to get the big lump of gold out the river, and how one of 'em was drownded for sure.

"How many of ye was there to start with?"

"Oh me!" says Pat. "There was seven 'fore that 'un got drownded. Poor feller!"

The man told him there were still seven. But they wouldn't believe him. Said they's already tried that countin' business themselves and they just knowed one of 'em was drownded. That man was about to go on, when a notion struck him. He was a real rascal and just couldn't resist the urge that came on him. He pointed to a ripe cowpile there in the road, about half dried-up, and he made all them Irishmen come and stand around it.

"You fellers all get down on your knees and stick your noses into that, and then count the holes your noses make, and you'll see."

So they all got down and stuck their noses in. Pat sat back and counted seven holes. Then they all counted to make sure, and all at once they started laughin'.

"We're all of us here! None of us poor fellers got drownded!"

So they thanked the man and on they went.

# *The Old Woman and Her Pig*

(England)

An old woman was sweeping her house, and she found a little crooked sixpence.

"What," said she, "shall I do with this little sixpence? I will go to market and buy a little pig."

As she was coming home, she came to a stile, but the piggy wouldn't go over the stile.

She went a little further, and she met a dog. So she said to him: "Dog! dog! bite pig; piggy won't go over the stile; and I shan't get home tonight." But the dog wouldn't.

She went a little further, and she met a stick. So she said: "Stick! stick! beat dog! dog won't bite pig; piggy won't get over the stile; and I shan't get home tonight." But the stick wouldn't.

She went a little further, and she met a fire. So she said: "Fire! fire! burn stick: stick won't beat dog; dog won't bite pig; piggy won't get over the stile; and I shan't get home tonight." But the fire wouldn't.

She went a little further, and she met some water. So she said: "Water! water! quench fire; fire won't burn stick; stick won't beat dog; dog won't bite pig; piggy won't get over the stile; and I shan't get home tonight." But the water wouldn't.

She went a little further, and she met an ox. So she said: "Ox! ox! drink water; water won't quench fire; fire won't burn stick; stick won't beat dog; dog won't bite pig; piggy won't get over the stile; and I shan't get home tonight." But the ox wouldn't.

She went a little further and she met a butcher. So she said: "Butcher! butcher! kill ox; ox won't drink water; water won't quench fire; fire won't burn stick; stick won't beat dog; dog won't bite pig; piggy won't get over the stile; and I shan't get home tonight." But the butcher wouldn't.

She went a little further and she met a rope. So she said: "Rope! rope! hang butcher; butcher won't kill ox; ox won't drink water; water won't quench fire; fire won't burn stick; stick won't beat dog; dog won't bite pig; piggy won't get over the stile; and I shan't get home tonight." But the rope wouldn't.

She went a little further and she met a rat. So she said: "Rat! rat! gnaw rope; rope won't hang butcher; butcher won't kill ox; ox won't drink water; water won't quench fire; fire won't burn stick; stick won't beat dog; dog won't bite pig; piggy won't get over the stile; and I shan't get home tonight." But the rat wouldn't.

She went a little further and she met a cat. So she said: "Cat! cat! kill rat; rat won't gnaw rope; rope won't hang butcher; butcher won't kill ox; ox won't drink water; water won't quench fire; fire won't burn stick; stick won't beat dog; dog won't bite pig; piggy won't get over the stile; and I shan't get home tonight." But the cat said to her, "If you will go to yonder cow and fetch me a saucer of milk, I will kill the rat." So away went the old woman to the cow.

But the cow said to her: "If you will go to yonder haystack and fetch me a handful of hay, I'll give you the milk." So away went the old woman to the haystack; and she brought the hay to the cow.

As soon as the cow had eaten the hay, she gave the old woman the milk; and away she went with it in a saucer to the cat.

As soon as the cat had lapped up the milk, the cat began to kill the rat; the rat began to gnaw the rope; the rope began to hang the butcher; the butcher began to kill the ox; the ox began to drink the water; the water began to quench the fire; the fire began to burn the stick; the stick began to beat the dog; the dog began to bite the pig; the little pig in a fright jumped over the stile; and so the old woman got home that night.

# *The Holmolaiset Build a House*

(Finland)

In a very remote part of Finland, there was a little village called Holmola. The people of Holmola, or the Holmolaiset, never traveled away from their town. They were happy there and had no need for anything else. Very seldom did anyone visit Holmola, so the people there became very set in their ways. You might even say they became quite different from the rest of the people in Finland. In fact, you might call them not only unique but weird. They became simple-minded and conservative.

Making decisions was extremely difficult for them as they pondered this way versus that way. They would talk, argue, discuss and consider things for weeks before they ever got around to any action.

The Holmolaiset were rather like stories told about the Wise Men of Gotham or the Fools of Chelm. They were unpredictable and managed to make easy jobs difficult. These noodleheads would follow an idea to its extremes.

At this particular time, the Holmolaiset were getting ready for a new project. Everyone was arguing with each other and raising a ruckus. It had been like this for a year. It was all because the people got tired of living in houses shaped like wigwams. After a lot of discussion they decided to build houses that were different. They wanted to make houses using logs.

They organized people into teams for the different jobs. One team of Holmolaiset would cut down the trees, another group would trim the branches off and another bunch would peel the bark off of the trees. Another man would take out his homemade tape measure and measure the trees for the right length. There were men whose job was to cut the tree into the measured lengths. As these men worked they were heard to mumble the craftsman rule, "measure twice, cut once." Yet another gang would carry the logs to the place where the house was to be built.

Two fellows notched the ends of the logs so they would fit together tightly. It took four more men to lift the logs into place to make the walls. Women came along and chinked the places where the logs rested on each other with moss. When all the walls were up, the roofing group got to work.

Once they had decided how they would get the work done, they all worked on it. Slowly they worked, but carefully, until the log house was done. Then the workers went inside the finished house and closed the door.

"What has gone wrong?" they asked. They hadn't ever counted on it being pitch-black dark inside. After all, wasn't this log house built in the sunshine? "We chinked all of the walls so the sunshine would stay inside and not leak out," said the women.

The people all gathered together to solve this problem. What had happened to the sunshine? Where had it gone? They started to blame each other for making a mistake that helped the sun escape.

They brought in their local wise man to fix things and get the sunlight back. The wizard drummed on his drum while he chanted and sung spells to bring back the sun. He was a good wizard—the best they had. But his songs and chants, spells, and drumming didn't change anything. It was still dark, dark, dark inside the house.

After several months of arguing, discussing, considering, and deciding, they felt that they had to carry sunlight into the house. This would be a very simple thing to do. All they had to do was to make great woolen sacks, fill them up with sunlight, twist the top of the sacks, and carry the sacks inside the house. Then they would open the sacks and let the sunlight fill the house.

Everyone worked hard to fill the house with sacks filled with sunlight, but when they went into the log building, closed the door and opened the bags, nothing happened. It was still dark, dark, dark inside the house.

Just at this time, a stranger named Matti happened to come to their town. Everyone was arguing and shouting. Matti asked them, "Is there something that I could help you with?"

The Holmolaiset told him what had happened and moaned about how everything had gone wrong, even after all of their careful planning.

"That's no problem, people of Holmola," declared Matti, "Where I come from we have been living in log houses with sunlight for a long time. I'll help you get the sunlight into the house if you pay me a thousand marks."

After a lot of loud bickering, the people of the village agreed.

"Fine," said Matti. "Watch what I do." he told them. He walked into the house, kept the door open so he could see, took his axe from his belt and chopped out a square hole in the wall. When he was done, the sun streamed into the house and gave enough light that everyone could see all the empty sacks they had used, lying on the earthen floor. Everyone was delighted. They paid Matti and thanked him for his idea and his help.

Matti continued on his trip and no sooner was he out of the village limits and heading into the forest than the people got to arguing again. Since Matti's idea had worked so well they decided to improve upon it. Before they had properly discussed, argued, considered, and thought of all the possibilities, they set about improving the house. They started to hack out more windows in the house. They cheered as they saw more sunshine stream in the house. These noodleheads cut so many windows that before you could say "crash," the whole roof came tumbling down on their heads.

And that is why you will never find a log cabin in Holmola even to this day. The Holmolaiset keep telling the story of the time they let more sunshine in the log house and everyone learned from the story. No log houses in Holmola!

# *Cuckoo in the Hedge*

(England)

It was a sparkling spring day and the cuckoo bird was singing in the meadows and woods. The people of Gotham were treated to a chorus of beauty starting at the crack of dawn. The role of the cuckoo bird was to herald spring and it was fulfilling its role.

Several of the men of Gotham were admiring the musical concert and one of them suggested, "Why don't we build a hedge around a cuckoo."

"What would we want to do that for?" questioned one of them.

"So we can hear them all year long," was the reply.

"That is a good idea," the men all said.

The workers had chosen a hedge on an ancient mound on a hill above the village, where the bird was, to build. They formed groups of Gothamites to cut trees, dig holes and put the timbers into the earth and the women did their share to help. They wove ropes of heather that were tied around the posts to make the structure sturdy. While they did all of this the cuckoo never moved from the hedge he was sitting on. He sat and sang.

"There now! That will keep our bird safe and let us hear his sweet song all the time," one of them said as the fence was finished. They stood back to appreciate the song of the bird and admire their handiwork.

"Not only will our fence enclose the bird, but it is a handsome piece of work," bragged another of the men of Gotham. As they stood, pleased with what they had done, the cuckoo flew away.

"The cuckoo has escaped! There it goes! Our fence failed. If only we had made the fence higher, she would not have escaped."

And so, to this day, you can see Cuckoo Bush Hill near Gotham. The fence that was raised to keep the bird singing all year long looks a bit weathered and bedraggled. Some say they have seen cuckoos fly into the hedge inside the fence to sit and sing their song of spring even today.

*This silly story comes from the village of Gotham, England.*

# *Gotham Arithmetic*

(England)

What happens on a crystal clear day in May? People everywhere think of other things to do than that which is their daily work. And so it was, on such a day, twelve men of Gotham agreed that it was a good day to go fishing. They gathered their fishing gear and took off for a brook with rapids and pools of calm water.

Some of the men went straight to wading in the waters while others stood on the banks and fished. They were happily and busily engaged in catching fish. "What a fine dinner we and our families will have tonight!" one of the men announced. All agreed with him.

It was a happy group of men who walked home with not a worry in the world nor anything but spring happiness. One of the men, as they walked, mused, "We all waded and gathered by the waters today. None of us drowned, did they?"

"Now that is a problem I did not consider," answered another man. "Let us count and make sure that all twelve of us are here." They all stood in a row and he began to count them. When he finished, he counted only eleven men because he had neglected to count himself.

"Alas," he cried. "One of us must have drowned."

Fat Ned looked and said, "Maybe you did not count right. I'll count this time." And so he did. When he finished, he also only counted eleven. The men became alarmed that one of them had most certainly drowned. Several of them even dissolved into salty tears and sniffles.

"Let's go back to the brook," one suggested so they did. They looked all over the banks they had fished from and walked upstream and downstream but they never found anything. Their grieving became louder with this.

While they stood helplessly, down the road came three men. One was Jack of Dover, Richard the alderman, and a courtier of King Richard. They were engaged in conversation about where they might locate the fool of fools since they all knew the men of Gotham were lacking. The king's man, on seeing the men along the shore of the water hailed them. "Are you men of Gotham? We hear this sorry group of men may not be really fools but instead they are playing the fool to fool the king."

"Woe to us, we care not about such things," wailed one of the fishermen. "One of us has drowned."

"How did this happen?" asked the alderman.

"Alas and alack. When we left to go fishing there were twelve of us and now there are only eleven. Someone has drowned!"

Jack of Dover looked around him and saw that there were twelve men present. "What makes you think one has drowned?" he asked.

"We have each counted and each time we found there were only eleven present," one of the fishermen wailed.

Richard squinted his eyes and asked, "You counted carefully?"

"Of course we did," countered Fat Ned. "Watch while I count again and you'll see that one of us is drowned." And so he counted again and as before, there were eleven men since he had not counted himself. "There," he cried, "there are only eleven of us."

The three men looked at each other. Jack of Dover pronounced, "To me, this is just foolery."

Richard told Jack to go back and tell King John about this.

Jack stood there and said again, "They are just playing the fool."

The king's courtier said, "I'll put an end to this." He turned to the men of Gotham and said, "What will you give me if I find the twelfth man?"

The men of Gotham looked at each other and agreed, "We will give you all the money we have."

"Then, it is time you gave me your money," the courtier said. The men of Gotham emptied their pockets and wallets and Jack and Richard just looked at them in amazement.

"Now," said the courtier, "stand in a line for me." This they did and the courtier came up the line and gave each one a hard blow on his shoulder. The blow was hard enough to make the fellow groan. "There is one," announced the courtier after he had struck the blow.

"This is the second," the courtier said as he struck another man. He went up the line of men and smacked each of them on their shoulder. When he hit the last man, with an extra hard smack, he cried, "And here is the twelfth one."

The men of Gotham stood in the row and rubbed their stinging shoulders but smiles soon came to their faces because they were all there. All twelve of them.

"Many thanks for finding our missing man," they said and then they went off down the road merrily.

"Well," said the courtier to Jack and the alderman, "certainly these men are the fools of fools for whom we have been looking. Then the three of them just shook their heads in amazement as they went on their way.

*Variants of this story are known in Russia, Scotland, India, and Iceland. It might seem that fools travel.*

# The Hummingbird

(China)

*Since Henny-penny never did make it to warn the king that the sky was a-falling, no one probably knows how the hummingbird clear over in China ever heard about the potential catastrophe.*

In the jungles of Asia there are many hummingbirds. They are of a variety of bright brilliant colors and people there refer to them as "flying jewels."

It was a hot, dampish day in the great China jungle. Elephant was placing one foot in front of another and swinging his trunk as he traveled down the trail. Suddenly this great beast saw a tiny bright hummingbird lying flat on its back on the ground.

The bird looked to be dead, for its two tiny feet were raised up into the air. It did not move at all; it just lay there with its feet pointing skyward.

The elephant moved close to the tiny bird and gave it a gentle nudge with his trunk.

"Do not push me around so," said the hummingbird.

"Then, you are not dead," said the worried elephant. "What on earth are you doing there like that!? You could get trampled."

The hummingbird opened his eyes to look up at the concerned elephant. "I have heard that the sky might fall today. If that is really what is going to happen, I am ready to do my bit and help hold it up."

The elephant couldn't help laughing at this tiny optimistic creature. His laughter turned to mockery. "Come now, little bird, do you really think that those tiny feet of yours could possibly hold up the sky?"

The little bird looked up at this giant beast and quietly admitted, "No I could not probably do it all by myself, but every creature must do what it can do. And, this is what I can do!"

# *Tricksters*

*Comedy is simply a funny way of being serious*

*Peter Ustinov*

# *Stone Soup*

(Ireland)

There was a poor, hungry, and cold, traveling man going on the road between green fields and villages. He had been traveling from village to village with his penny whistle and Irish harp, making music, and money, along the way.

One day as he was trudging down the road, all he could think of was how good a bowl of hot soup would be. In fact, he knew that a bowl of good soup would fix everything that was wrong with him at that moment.

As he was passing by a farmer's house, he got the great idea that the wife of the farmer there would help him out with his hunger problem. He decided to try his luck. He went down to the shore of the river and picked up a round river stone about the size of a large apple. He went to the farmer's house, knocked on the door, and was pleased when his knock was answered by the wife.

"Dear woman," he said, "would you give me a pan and a small drop of clean warm water?"

The wife was as kind as he hoped she would be and she did as he asked. He started to wash and clean the stone with great splashing and ceremony until the stone was shining clean.

The wife was curious and told him, "You have certainly done a grand job of washing that stone."

"And why not, kind lady? It is my very special soup stone," he replied. "Not only can I make soup with it, but it will be the best soup," the man said as he fondly rubbed the stone.

"Mercy be to the heaven! How could anyone do that?" she asked.

"There would be no trouble at all to it," he bragged. "All a person would have to do is to watch the one who knows how to make stone soup."

"Oh my, oh my!" she exclaimed. "I would be extremely pleased to watch you do it. There is the pot and there is the fire, and there is plenty of water," she told him as she led him into the cozy kitchen.

Things were working out just as he had planned. The man put a half gallon of water in the pot and ceremoniously placed the stone in the water. The two of them stood by the bubbling pot and watched it. Then, the fellow sat down on one of the kitchen chairs, took up his Irish harp and started strumming a song and singing along with it.

A couple of local people heard the music as they were coming down the road and stopped by the kitchen door to see what was happening.

"You know, kind woman," the harpist said as he saw the faces in the door, "a shake of salt and pepper would not do it any harm."

She gave the salt and pepper to him and he made a great show of measuring out just the right amount. Now the faces belonging to the fellows in the doorway, were familiar ones to the good wife.

"And what brings you two here after all of your unpleasant actions lately?" she asked.

"Oh, dear Maggie, we came to say we are sorry, to listen to the music, and to see if there is anything we can do to make things better," one answered.

The harpist took the chance to suggest, "We are making some soup. It could stand the bone of a leg of mutton for flavor."

"Maggie, to show you how sorry we are, we will go home and get our wives to come help and we will bring a sturdy meat covered bone back with us."

The frown that was on Maggie's face disappeared, and she answered, "Your apologies are accepted as well as your offer of a meaty bone."

Off the two men went. The harpist turned to the wife and said, "A good handful of white flour would help thicken the soup right now."

She got such a handful and came back to put it right into the pot herself. The fellow sat down with his harp again and played some merry music.

The two fellows returned with their wives and the mutton bone. That was added to the soup and the three women began to talk with each other like there had never been a problem between them. "That's a fine bone," said the harpist. "There is plenty of meat on it and it will make the soup much stronger." And then as if he were musing to himself, "A few potatoes would give it great texture."

One of the wives said, "I can go back to our cottage and get some potatoes."

Not to be outdone, the other wife said, "Maybe a few fine onions would help. I'll get some from our neighbor's garden and bring them back with me."

The potatoes and onions came along with several more people. From what the people were saying, there had been some misunderstandings in the recent past but they were all being forgotten as the women sat down together to peel the potatoes and chop them up and add them to the soup. The onions were sliced and cut and added.

All the harpist had to do at this point was to make more merry music and sing as people added to the pot. It was starting to smell really wonderful by now, but one of the newcomers said, "It needs some carrots and turnips. I'll go borrow some from Mary. Maybe she and her family will want to join us."

Off she went and quickly returned with more people and the carrots and turnips, which were cleaned, chopped, and added to the soup. The soup bubbled and boiled merrily for a little bit longer. The musician played some sentimental songs, and they all joined along in singing as he played.

Pretty soon this gathering of people had forgotten all of their quibbles and was mellow with the music, and the smell of soup. The man of the house returned from work and was amazed to see who all was in his home getting along so well together.

The musician stopped playing, jumped up, and got a spoon. He handed it to the husband and said, "You should be the one to taste the soup. What do you think of it?"

"Yes, dear husband, this is special soup made with a special stone to give it flavor."

The husband sipped the soup off the spoon and declared it delicious. "This is truly fine soup but maybe I need to have another taste to make sure," and he dipped the spoon into the soup to get another spoonful.

Quickly, bowls and spoons appeared and everyone there sipped, slurped and slowly enjoyed bowls of the soup. The rascally musician played more music and all the guests were full of good will and happiness.

The housewife said, "I am extremely grateful to you for showing me how to make such good soup."

"What did I tell you?" said the harpist. "I knew that you could make nothing but the finest, richest soup with my special stone."

After the soup was gone, the men set back and lit pipes of tobacco and enjoyed a good smoke together. "It's been a long time since we have done this together," one of the men said to the others.

The traveling musician played a final merry melody on his penny whistle and resumed his travels.

The housewife never stopped bragging about how she could make soup with a stone. All the neighbors complimented her on its discovery. I think it is safe to say that the people enjoyed each other's fine company after that, and it was probably a long time before the man came back to that part of Ireland again.

# *The Cat and The Mouse*

(Germany)

The cat, having made acquaintance with a mouse, pretended such great love for her that the mouse agreed that they should live and keep house together.

"We must make provisions for the winter," said the cat, or "we shall suffer hunger, and you, little mouse, must not stir out or you will be caught in a trap."

So they took counsel together and bought a little pot of fat. Then they had a problem as to where to put it for safety. After long consideration, the cat said there could not be a better place than the church, for nobody would steal there. Cat said they should put it under the altar and not touch it until they were really in want. So, this was done and the little pot placed in safety.

But before long, the cat was seized with a great wish to taste it.

"Listen to me, little mouse," said he, "I have been asked by my cousin to stand god-father to a little son she has brought into the world. He is white with brown spots and they want to have the christening today. Let me go to it and you stay at home and keep house."

"Oh yes, certainly," answered the mouse. "Pray go, by all means and when you are feasting on all the good things, think of me. I should so like a drop of the sweet red wine."

But there was not a word of truth in all this. The cat had no cousin, and had not been asked to stand as god-father. He went to the church, straight up to the little pot, and licked the fat off the top. Then he took a walk over the roofs of the town, saw his acquaintances, stretched himself in the sun, and licked his whiskers as often as he thought of the little pot of fat, and when it was evening he went home.

"Here you are at last," said the mouse. "I expect you have had a merry time."

"Oh, pretty well," answered the cat.

"And what name did you give the child?" asked the mouse.

"Top-off," answered the cat, dryly.

"Top-off," cried the mouse. "That is a singular and wonderful name! Is it common in your family?"

"What does it matter?" said the cat. "It's not any worse than Crumb-picker, like your god-child."

A little time after this, the cat was again seized with a longing.

"Again, I must ask you," said he to the mouse, "to do me a favor and keep house alone for a day. I have been asked a second time to stand god-father. The little one has a white ring round its neck. I cannot well refuse."

So the kind little mouse consented, and the cat crept along by the town wall until he reached the church, and going straight to the little pot of fat, devoured half of it. "Nothing tastes so well as what one keeps to oneself," said he, feeling quite content with his day's work.

When he reached home, the mouse asked what name had been given to the child.

"Half-gone," answered the cat.

"Half-gone!" cried the mouse. "I have never heard such a name in my life! I'll bet it's not to be found in the calendar."

Soon after that, the cat's mouth began to water again for the fat.

"Good things always come in threes," said he to the mouse. "Again I have been asked to stand as god-father. The little one is quite black with white feet and not any white hair on its body. Such a thing does not happen every day, so you will let me go, won't you?"

"Top-off, Half-gone," murmured the mouse. "They are such curious names I cannot but wonder at them!"

"That's because you are always sitting at home," said the cat. "In your little gray frock and hairy tail, never seeing the world, and fancying all sorts of things."

So the little mouse cleaned up the house and set it all in order. Meanwhile the greedy cat went and made an end of the little pot of fat.

"Now all is finished, one's mind will be easy," said he and came home in the evening, quite sleep and comfortable.

The mouse asked at once what name had been given to the third child. "It won't please you any better than the others," answered the cat. "It is called All-gone."

"All-gone!" cried the mouse. "What an unheard-of name! I never met with anything like it! All-gone! Whatever can it mean?" And shaking her head, she curled herself around and went to sleep. After that the cat was not again asked to stand god-father.

When the winter had come and there was nothing more to be had out of doors, the mouse began to think of their store.

"Come, eat," said she. "We will fetch our pot of fat. How good it will taste to be sure!"

"Of course it will," said the cat. "Just as good as if you stuck your tongue out of the window!"

So they went out and when they reached the place, they found the pot, but it was standing empty.

"Oh, now I know what it all meant," cried the mouse. "Now I see what sort of a partner you have been! Instead of standing god-father, you have devoured it all up. First, Top-off, then Half-gone, then. . ."

"Will you hold your tongue!" screamed the cat. "Another word and I will devour you too!"

And the poor little mouse, having "All-gone" on her tongue, out it came and the cat leaped upon her and made an end of her. Well, that is the way of the world.

*This story was collected by the Brothers Grimm.*

# *Cool Ride in the Sky*

(Caribbean Islands)

Everyone on the islands grew up hearing a story that was told back in Africa. The story starts out in the middle of the jungle in Africa on one hot, hot, hot day. Monkey was sitting up on the branch of a tree just looking around him. That was about all he could do since it was another hot day just like yesterday and the day before that, and the day before that, and the day before that.

Down in the clearing, Monkey could see all the small creatures that lived there just sitting beside the holes leading to their homes. Funniest of all, he thought, was the rabbit beside his hole. Poor rabbit was obviously suffering from the heat. There wasn't one hop left in him as he sat there with his ears dragging down to the ground and his little pink tongue hanging out. His nose was even motionless. That's how hot it was.

Then Monkey looked off in the sky and saw a black speck a long ways away. As he watched, it got closer and closer until he could see that it was a buzzard. Buzzard soared and circled slowly. It was around breakfast time and Monkey thought that buzzard was out looking for breakfast. The buzzard spotted the rabbit and circled in the air above him as he glided lower and lower and landed on the ground.

Rabbit looked alarmed, but was too uncomfortably hot to dive right away down into his hole. Buzzard sat there and looked at rabbit.

"What are you doing rabbit?" the buzzard asked.

"I am trying to decide if I should jump down into my hole and escape your clutches, but it is so hot I wish you would just fly off and leave me alone," rabbit begged.

"Why poor rabbit. Are you hot?" asked buzzard.

"Of course I am hot," answered rabbit as he started to move backwards slowly toward his hole.

"Maybe I have the answer for you. You know, when you fly in the sky the breezes keep you quite comfortable. I hardly notice the heat when I am soaring and sailing," smiled buzzard. "Maybe you should jump on my back and I will take you for a cool ride in the sky."

Rabbit thought about it and buzzard was certainly right. There had been no breezes of any kind lately and a good breeze would be quite welcome.

"But how do I know you aren't just trying to trick me?" he asked.

"Why rabbit, I promise you a cool ride in the sky. How can that be a trick?" replied buzzard.

So, rabbit slowly and carefully went over to buzzard. "I accept your offer," he said as he climbed up on buzzard's back.

"Now hang on securely," buzzard instructed rabbit. "Ready? Here we go."

Buzzard took a few leaps, spread his wings and took off for the flight. Sure enough, rabbit had to admit, it was cool riding in the sky. He could look down at all the other creatures suffering in the heat and enjoy the breezes as buzzard soared and sailed.

"It is time to go back down now," declared buzzard. He began to circle back to the earth but instead of slowing down, he flew fast. When he reached the ground, he did it in a steep drop and landed with a jerk that sent the rabbit flying solo into a rock. Buzzard went over to rabbit's body and settled down to enjoy his breakfast.

Monkey had seen it all and knew buzzard had planned ahead for his gourmet breakfast.

When the sun was straight overhead in the sky and blazing down on the forest and the clearing, Monkey was again sitting on his favorite branch. Again, his eye caught a dark speck in the sky that sailed, soared and circled close to the forest. To Monkey's surprise, buzzard landed on a branch of one of the tallest trees. Then, Monkey noticed a squirrel sitting beside his hole in the trunk of that tree.

"Hello squirrel," greeted buzzard. "What are you doing this fine day?"

Squirrel was suffering from the noon day heat and looked at buzzard, "What do you think I am doing? I am trying to survive this heat. Since you are here, I must get into the safety of my hole in the tree."

"Why do that?" asked buzzard. "If you are hot, I know a fine way for you to cool off."

"What might that be?" asked squirrel with a sneer. "It is worse to be dead than hot, and I don't trust you."

"Oh my, squirrel. I was only going to suggest something for you to relieve the heat. I thought you might want to climb on my back and go for a cool ride in the sky. You know a lovely breeze would help cool a furry squirrel like you," oozed buzzard.

"That is probably quite true, but I suspect you of trickery," said squirrel.

"I promise you no trickery, only a cool ride in the sky. But if you aren't interested, I'll say goodbye."

Squirrel sat outside his hole and thought about how things did get cooler the higher he got in the tree.

"You promise?" he asked.

"I promise you a cool ride in the sky, squirrel," stated the buzzard.

"All right," squirrel agreed. He carefully climbed over to the buzzard and climbed up on his back.

"Ready squirrel?" buzzard asked. "Make sure you hang on so you won't fall off." With that he jumped off the tree limb and started to glide, spread his wings, flapped them to gain some speed and soared, sailed, circled, and flew high in the sky.

"You were so right," said squirrel. "This is so comfortable flying like this in the breeze."

After a while, buzzard instructed squirrel, "Hang on. We are going down for a landing." Buzzard started to circle lower and lower but he never slowed down his speed; and then he went into a steep dive and landed so hard that squirrel lost his grip and flew on his own to the ground into the trunk of the tree. He was knocked out from the jolt.

Buzzard glided over to squirrel and ate him for lunch.

Monkey had seen all of this and figured out that buzzard planned to use a cool ride in the sky again when supper time came. He made his own plan.

Sure enough, at supper time as the sun was sinking in the sky, there was the speck of black sailing in. This time things were different. Monkey was on the ground in the middle of the clearing dancing. This caught buzzard's attention and he floated down near Monkey.

"What on earth are you doing?" buzzard demanded of Monkey.

"That's easy. I am doing a cool dance to celebrate the sun going down and then things will cool down. It has been a really hot day you know," explained Monkey.

Sure enough, buzzard gently replied. "So you have been hot today and are hoping to cool down? Well, I know how you can get cool right now without dancing and sweating, waiting for the sun to go down. You could hop on my back and I will take you up into the sky and give you a really cool ride."

"Sure," gasped Monkey as he continued to dance. "And what trick do you have up your feathers? You have never been kind to me before." demanded Monkey.

"Really Monkey, don't be so suspicious. I only offer you a chance for a cool ride in the evening sky," said buzzard.

"Well, that sounds like it might be a good idea," smiled Monkey. "Here I come."

Monkey left off his dancing and went over to buzzard and climbed onto his back. "Are you ready?" asked buzzard. "Make sure you have a good hold on my back so you don't fall off and here we go."

With that, buzzard made a graceful takeoff and slowly climbed into the sky where he once more glided, floated, soared, and sailed with Monkey on his back. They flew around and then buzzard said, "Well Monkey, you are heavy now and it is time to go back down." Then buzzard tried to throw Monkey off his back.

With that, Monkey grabbed buzzard around the neck and then carefully wrapped his tail tightly around the neck and said, "Straighten up and fly right, cool down papa, don't you blow your top. You know buzzard, it might be a great idea if you flew low and slow around the clearing so I can greet all of my friends down there."

The buzzard had no choice but to be humiliated and follow Monkey's directions. Monkey joyfully waved and shouted to all the creatures in the clearing. Buzzard was happy to fly off in disgrace when Monkey let loose his hold of hands and tail from his neck. Buzzard didn't have Monkey for supper that night.

Listen carefully to monkeys. On hot days it really seems as if you can hear them singing the song taught to them by Monkey. "Straighten up and fly right, ain't no use in divin', What's the use in jivin', straighten up and fly right, cool down papa, don't you blow your top."

*Nat King Cole grew up hearing this story and that is where his song "Straighten Up and Fly Right" came from.*

# *King of the Frogs*

(Tibet)

High in the great mountains of Tibet, a hungry tiger prowled in search of food. He wasn't having much luck because the rumbling of his empty stomach kept warning off his prey until he came upon a frog practicing high leaps on the river bank.

The frog caught sight of the hunter stalking him and knew it was too late for escape. "If I don't think extraordinarily fast," he told himself, "I shall be reduced to frog sauce in a moment's crunch."

The frog feigned unconcern and hopped onto a grassy mound, sat down, and raised his nose grandiloquently towards the sky. He looked every inch a frog that feared nothing under the heavens. Even when the tiger gave a deep growl, he didn't deign to look around.

The frog's manner gave the tiger pause. No frog had ever seemed so full of confidence as this one.

"Er... I do beg your pardon, poor frog, for disturbing your serenity, but I have not eaten for two days, and I must sustain myself on your flesh before I can seek bigger game. Normally, of course, I should not bother with such a small morsel as you, nor am I overly fond of frog in any case. I intend no offense, just a quick meal."

The frog continued to look at the heavens, but he bulged out his stomach and filled it as full as he could with air, and laughed his heartiest, deepest, croakiest laugh.

"Let me see, tiger, isn't it? Oh yes. Well tiger, I am the king of frogs and there is not one of your kind up to the chore of eating me, for I possess skills you cannot even imagine. However, because of your great hunger. . .," and he cast a sidelong glance at the tiger, "Dear, dear, you are quite thin, aren't you, poor thing well, then, I'll give you a chance to prove yourself greater than I, in which case I shall become your tasty morsel after all." The frog gave a lofty nod towards the river. "I say that I can leap the river faster than you. Is it a contest?"

The tiger smiled a shiny-toothed smile, and big drool of saliva spilled from his jaw. "I can scarcely lose. Prepare yourself to be eaten frog." He turned to face the river, tensing for a mighty leap.

As the big yellow and black tail swished over him, the frog closed his mouth on the tip at the very moment the tiger left the ground.

Landing with ease on the other bank of the river, the tiger whirled to look back across the water, "Ho frog!" he cried, "and where does that jump leave you?"

The frog, regaining his breath from the dizzying ride on the tiger's tail and choking slightly on the tiger hair in his throat, began to laugh. "You'll never find me looking in that direction, my slow friend."

The tiger whirled round. There behind him on a rock sat the frog observing the heavens as grandly as before.

"Not that yours wasn't a fine jump for a tiger," the frog continued. "Really, you know, I sat here and watched with great admiration as you came flying across to join me."

The tiger scowled fiercely and put out his paw, all the claws extended.

"Never mind," said the frog quickly. "We'll have another contest, one that will be fairer to you. Let me see. . . Ah, yes, there is coughing-up! I propose a coughing-up contest. With the magnificent size of your stomach, you can surely win over such a small bag of groats as mine."

On sure ground, the tiger nodded agreement. He drew in his stomach until it rubbed his backbone, and then coughed out onto the bank only a few globules of bile, for he had not eaten in two days. Frowning, he lifted his head.

The frog cleared his throat with a tiny cough and deposited on the ground a small hairball. He looked down at it disparagingly. "Not very much, I'm afraid. But it was yesterday that I last ate. I remember now. I was playing along the river when I saw a tiger coming for water. A sudden hunger struck me, so I er. . . This bit of hair is all that is left, I'm afraid."

The tiger stood staring at the frog. King of the frogs, indeed! King of the river bank! King of the mountain and of the plain!

Tail between his legs, the tiger made off as fast as he could, with many a backward look to be sure the frog was not following. In this manner, he almost ran over his friend the fox, who was coming down to the river to drink.

"What troubles you brother tiger?" asked the fox. "Truly it must be a great peril to put you in such a state."

The tiger panted out his story of meeting the King Frog.

The fox gave a short bark of derision. "King Frog! That's ridiculous. I shall have that pompous little croaker for breakfast! Come along, then, and I'll show you how to catch and swallow a rascal frog."

"You don't know! You can't imagine!" The tiger nervously rubbed his twitching ear with the back of one paw. "You will run away with fright, and I shall be left alone with the terrible monster!"

"Not I," said the fox. "Let's go and find this fine king."

"Only if we tie our tails together," the tiger insisted stubbornly. "That will unite our strengths. Besides making sure that you don't run away without me."

Rolling his eyes upward, the fox agreed, and so it was that with their tails tied firmly together, tiger and fox padded down the mountain to the river.

The frog was sitting in kingly dignity on top of his rock when they reached the river bank.

"Ho!" he shouted. "It's high time you came with your tribute. You good-for-nothing fox! What have you brought for my dinner today? Is it that old raggedy thing tied to your tail?"

Alarm rang through the tiger's head like ten thousand gongs. His poor hungry head! How stupid he was! He had fallen directly into the traitor fox's trap! If he didn't escape forthwith, he would end up as one small hairball coughed out of the frog's throat.

With a great twisting turn, he sprang into the air and, fleeing, scarcely put paw to ground until he was far up in the mountains. At last he dropped with exhaustion and lay for a long time recovering his breath. Only then did he realize that his tail was still tied to the tail of his once-friend, the fox, and that the worthy creature was quite dead.

"Woe is me! What will King Frog do next?" quivered the great hungry tiger in terror!

# *The Huge Turnip*

(Poland)

There were once two brothers who both served as soldiers, one of them was rich, and the other poor. The poor one, to escape from his poverty, took off his soldier's coat and burned it, and became a farmer. He dug and hoed his bit of land, and sowed it with turnip seed. The seed came up, and one turnip grew there which became large and vigorous, and visibly grew bigger and bigger. It seemed as if it would never stop growing, so that it might have been called the princess of turnips. Never before was such a one seen, and never will such a one be seen again.

It finally became so enormous that it filled a whole cart, and two oxen were required to draw it, and the farmer had not the least idea what he was to do with the turnip. Would it be a fortune to him or a misfortune? At last he thought, "If I sell it, what will I get for it? If I eat it myself, why the small turnips would taste just as good. It would be better to take it to the King, and make him a present of it."

So he placed it on a cart, harnessed two oxen, took it to the palace and presented it to the king. "What strange thing is this?" asked the king. "Many wonderful things have come before my eyes, but never such a monster as this! From what seed can this huge turnip have sprung, or are you a lucky child and have met with it by chance?"

"Ah, no!" said the farmer. "No lucky child am I. I am a poor soldier, who, because he could no longer support himself hung his soldier's coat on a nail and took to farming land. I have a brother who is rich and well known to you. There's one of my problems, I have nothing, so I am forgotten by everyone."

The king felt compassion for him and told him, "You shall be raised from poverty, and shall have such gifts from me that you shall be equal to your rich brother." Then he bestowed on him much gold, and lands, and meadows, and herds, and made him immensely rich, so that the wealth of the other brother could not be compared with his.

When the rich brother heard what the poor one had gained for himself with one single turnip, he envied him, and thought in every way how he also could get hold of a similar piece of luck. He would, however, set about it in a much wiser way, and took gold and horses and carried them to the king. He made certain the king would give him a much larger present in return. If his brother had gotten so much for one turnip, what would he not carry away with him in return for such beautiful things as these? The king accepted his presents, and said he had nothing to give him in return that was more rare and excellent than the great turnip.

So the rich man was obliged to put his brother's turnip in a cart and have it taken to his home. Once there he did not know on whom to vent his rage and anger, until bad thoughts came to him. He resolved to kill his brother. He hired murderers, who were to lie in ambush. Then he went to his brother and said, "Dear brother, I know of a hidden treasure. We will dig it up together, and divide it between us."

The other agreed to this and accompanied him without suspicion. While they were on their way, however, the murderers fell on him, bound him and would have hanged him to a tree. Just as they were doing this, loud singing and the sound of a horse's feet were heard in the distance. On this their hearts were filled with terror, and they pushed their prisoner head first into the sack, hung it on a branch, and took flight. He, however, worked up there until he had made a hole in the sack through which he could put his head.

The man who was coming by was no other than a traveling student. He was just a young fellow who rode on his way through the wood joyously singing his song. When he who was aloft saw that someone was passing below him, he cried, "Good day! You have come at a lucky time."

The student looked around on every side but did not know from where the voice came. At last he said, "Who calls me?"

An answer came from the top of the tree. "Raise your eyes. Here I sit aloft in the Sack of Wisdom. In a short time have I learned great things. Compared with this, all schools are just a waste of time. In a very short time I shall have learned everything and shall descend wiser than all other men. I understand the stars and the signs of the zodiac, and the tracks of the winds, the sand of the sea, the healing of illness, and the virtues of all herbs, birds, and stones. If you were once within it you would feel what noble things issue forth from the Sack of Knowledge."

The student, when he heard all of this, was astonished and said, "Blessed be the hour in which I have found you! May not I also enter the sack for a while?"

He who was above replied as if unwillingly. "For a short time I will let you get into it. If you reward me and give me good words, but you must wait an hour longer. There is one thing that remains which I must learn before I do it."

When the student had waited a while, he became impatient and begged to be allowed to get in at once. His thirst for knowledge was so very great.

He who was above pretended at last to yield and said, "In order that I may come forth from the house of knowledge, you must let it down by the rope. Then you shall enter it."

So the student let the sack down, untied it, and set him free. Then he cried, "Now draw me up at once," and was about to get into the sack. "Halt!" said the other, "that won't do." He took him by the head and put him upside down into the sack, fastened it, and drew the disciple of wisdom up the tree by the rope. Then he swung him in the air and said, "How goes it with you, my dear fellow? Behold, already you feel wisdom coming, and are gaining valuable experience. Keep perfectly quiet until you become wiser."

Thereupon, he mounted the student's horse and rode away. In an hours time though, he sent someone to let the student out again.

# *To Those Who Know—To Those Who Don't*

(Persia)

*This is one of many humorous stories about the character Nasruddin of Persia, which is now Iran.*

One day Mulla Nasruddin went to the mosque to preach. He climbed the minbar (the Muslim pulpit) and asked the congregation, "Do you know or do you not know?"

"We do not know," they responded in unison.

"I have naught to reveal to ignoramuses," he remarked as he left the mosque.

Next day he got up the minbar and repeated the question, "Do you know or do you not know?"

"We surely know," they replied.

"In that case I have nothing to reveal to you," he said and left the mosque.

The third day when he returned and got up the minbar, his congregation had gotten wise to him. When he raised the question again, "Do you know or do you not know?" half the congregation replied, "We know," while the other half responded, "We do not know."

"In that case," said Nasruddin, "will those who know share their wisdom with those who do not know?" and left the mosque.

# *The Brahman's Goat*

(India)

A Brahman named Friendly, lived in a small town where he had undertaken the task of maintaining the sacred fire. It was in the month of February and a gentle breeze was blowing. The sky was veiled in clouds and a drizzling rain fell. The Brahman went to another village to beg a victim for the necessary sacrifice and said, "Oh sacrificer, I wish to make an offering on the approaching day of the new moon. I ask you to give me a victim."

The man gave the Brahman a plump goat, just as the scripture prescribed. The Brahman placed the goat on his shoulder and started for his own city in great haste.

On the road he met three rogues whose throats were pinched and dry from hunger. These three saw the plump goat on the Brahman's shoulder and whispered to each other, "Come now! If we could eat that creature, we should have the laugh on this miserable weather. Let us fool that Brahman, get the goat and fill our bellies."

So, the first of them changed his clothes and took a shortcut to meet the Brahman further up the road. "Oh pious Brahman, why are you doing such a thing that is so unconventional and ridiculous? You are carrying an unclean animal, a dog, on your shoulder. Are you ignorant of the verse:

*The dog and the rooster,*
*The hangman, the ass,*

*The camel, defile you;*
*Don't touch them, but pass.*

Anger mastered the Brahman when he heard this. "Are you blind man, that you declare dog-hood to a goat?"

"Do not be angry Brahman," said the man. "Continue on your journey."

When the Brahman had traveled a little farther, the second rogue met him and declared, "Alas, hold sir, alas! Even if this dead calf was a pet, still you should not put it on your shoulder. The proverb says:"

*Touch not unwisely man or beast*
*That lifeless lie:*
*Else, gifts of milk and lunar fast*
*Must purify.*

Then the Brahman spoke in anger. "Are you blind man? You call a goat a calf!"

The rogue replied, "Holy man, do not be angry. I spoke in ignorance. Do as you will."

When the Brahman had walked only a little further through the forest, the third rogue, in different clothes, met him and said, "Sir, this is most improper. Improper, indeed. You are carrying a donkey on your shoulder and the proverb tells us:"

*If you should touch an ass—be it*
*In ignorance or not—*
*You needs must wash your clothes and bathe,*
*To cleanse the sinful spot.*

"Pray drop this thing before another person might see you."

So the Brahman concluded that it was a goblin in quadruped form, threw the animal on the ground and made for home. He was terrified.

Meanwhile, the three rogues met, caught the goat and carried out their eager plan. And so, the strong, deft, clever rascals noted how they had robbed the Brahman of his goat.

# *Tyll Ulenspiegel*

(Belgium)

Tyll Ulenspiegel, the prankster, was always telling people the truth through jests and pranks. His jests were always directed against the mean, the stingy, the cruel, and the deceitful. This was the case in the dukedom of Luxembourg many ages ago.

He had ridiculed the Duke of Luxembourg until the Duke threatened to hang Tyll if he ever came to his dukedom again. That didn't deter Tyll. He roamed throughout the country but was careful to avoid meeting its ruler.

"I don't think hanging is something I want to do anytime soon," he said.

And then it happened. The Duke's men caught Tyll, but he had seen them coming and had his horse lay down. Tyll stood on the stomach of his horse and when the Duke's men came to capture him, Tyll roared, "I am protected by the law of the land." The law of the land involved the fact that a man could not be taken or hurt while he was within the four posts of his domicile. "See my horse with his four legs in the air? I am standing on his stomach and therefore am in my own home."

When the Duke's men reported this to him, the Duke said, "Tyll wins again this time but he must not show his face in my land again. He will certainly hang."

This warning did worry Tyll. If the truth were told, Tyll enjoyed danger and adventure. He never avoided them. And so, one day he was riding in a cart pulled by his horse through the dukedom.

He knew it was just a matter of time until he tangled up again with the Duke's men, so he stopped his horse beside a field where a man was plowing.

"Who does this land you are plowing belong to?" asked Tyll.

"It was my father's, his father's, and his father's, and now it is mine." was the answer.

"Ho, my good man. What do you want for a cartful of your land?" Tyll asked.

"Now that is an interesting request. I have never considered it before but I guess a shilling would do for it," mused the farmer.

"Then it will be done," stated Tyll. He gave the man a shilling and the farmer even helped Tyll fill his cart with the dirt from his field. Tyll thanked him and gathered the reins to his horse and rode away.

Hardly had he done this when at a turn in the road he met the Duke and his men. They chased after Tyll and were surprised when they caught up to find Tyll up to his neck in the earth in his cart.

"Didn't I forbid you to set foot on my land under penalty of hanging," demanded the Duke as he looked at Tyll quizzically.

"Ah, my wise, gracious ruler. I am not on your land. I happen to be on my own land. I bought it for a shilling from a peasant back along the road. The land had been in his family for generations. Therefore, this is my land!" bragged Tyll.

Even the Duke could not help himself and he joined his men in laughter. "Tyll," he warned, "keep off my land. Even if you stand on your own cart of land, you are on my land. If you persist in your pranks, I will have no choice but to conquer your land and after I have done that, I will hang you as an enemy," he said with cold eyes looking at Tyll. "Remember, you must not come on my lands again."

Tyll quickly went on his way but as a final gift to the Duke, he left his earth as a present on the ground just before the bridge that led to the castle. Some say, that earth is still there today as a reminder that Tyll Ulenspiegel had enjoyed his jests with the Duke.

# *The Night It Rained Bagels*

(Russia)

There were two brothers who lived in a small Russian village. The older brother was named Igor and the younger one was called Boris. Igor was very clever and cunning, while Boris was good, trusting and simple-minded.

Igor worked hard growing things in the family fields. Meanwhile Boris took care of the house, baked, and cooked their meals. They worked together in pleasant comfort. Each needed the other.

One day as Igor was out in the fields plowing new ground with his team of oxen and a plow, he dug up a pot of gold. Never before had he seen such riches! There was only one problem. He knew that Boris would never be able to keep such riches a secret. Boris would immediately tell everyone he saw about their good fortune.

Igor thought, "If I bring the gold home, Boris will tell the neighbors and they will tell the master of the manor and he will promptly take it from us." There in the middle of the partly plowed field Igor thought about this problem. He sat down on the ground and ran the gold through his fingers and puzzled over what to do.

"I know what I will do!" he exclaimed to the oxen. He immediately got up, ran home for a shovel, ran back to the field, and buried the pot of gold. He marked the spot where the gold was with a rock and then he took the oxen back to their stalls.

Igor's plan was becoming clearer to him now. He went to the brook that ran through their farm and took out the net he had strung across the stream in the morning. Sure enough! There was a fish in it. He took the fish and went to his fox trap. He took the fox out of the trap and put the fish in its place. Next he took the fox to the brook and put it into the fishnet.

Igor was smiling to himself as he entered the kitchen. "Boris, make us some bagels for supper," he said.

"No one eats bagels for supper," replied Boris as he scratched his head.

"Well then, let's be different. We shall," announced Igor. "And after we eat the bagels for supper and it is dark we must hurry to the field where I found a pot of gold. We'll have to bring the gold home in the dark."

Boris mixed up the bagels and got a pan of water boiling to cook them in. When he had made the bagels, Igor sat down at the table and ate the bagels Boris had made. For every bagel Igor ate he put two of them in his bag.

When the bag was full, Igor told Boris, "I have had enough. I am full. I will go to the field now. Finish eating your bagels and catch up with me." Igor took up a lantern and went outside. Instead of going straight to the field, he went to the trees in the orchard. He took the bagels out of his bag and hung them on the trees and then went to the spot in the field where he had buried the pot of gold.

Boris caught up with him on the way to the field and told Igor in amazement, "Look at the trees! There are bagels growing on the trees. I have never seen bagels grow on trees. I didn't know bagels grew on trees. It would have been easier for me to pick bagels from the trees than to go through all the bother of cooking them."

"You are being silly," said Igor. "Everyone knows that bagels do not grow on trees." To make further fun of his brother, Igor said, "Maybe it was the bagel cloud that just passed overhead. The bagels must have rained down from the cloud!"

Then Igor told Boris, "My fox trap is nearby. Let's go and see if I have caught any of those chicken-eating foxes."

They walked to the fox trap and Boris was full of wonder because there was a fish in the trap. "How on earth could a fish get into the trap?" puzzled Boris.

"That's easy. There are fish that walk on the ground. Didn't you know that? This is one of the biggest of them I have ever seen," said Igor.

Boris was still puzzled as he tried to think about what a fish that walked on the ground looked like. "I never knew about that," he said.

They went to the brook and Boris said, "Let's see if there is anything in the net." He reached out to where the net was pegged into the ground and pulled out the net. To his surprise there was a fox in it. "What is happening today?" Boris cried. "I have never seen a fox in a fishnet before!"

"Silly Boris," said his brother. "Haven't you ever seen water foxes before? How long have you lived here and never seen water foxes before?"

They crossed over into the field and Igor took the shovel from his backpack and dug up the pot of gold. It gleamed and glowed by the lantern light. Together they started to carry it home. They had to go past the master's house. Inside the sheep pen some sheep were bleating. "Meeee! Meeee! Meeee!"

"Oh Igor! What is that noise? I am frightened," whispered Boris.

"Run, run, run as fast as you can! The devil is whipping the master. Run fast before the devil finds us here and whips us too," urged Igor.

Boris didn't need any urging. He flew home as fast as he could. Igor was carrying the pot of gold along with him and he didn't seem to go too fast. When they got home Boris was panting in terror. Meanwhile, Igor hid the gold. "Remember," Igor told Boris, "don't say a word to anyone or we will be in trouble. Don't tell anyone! You must keep this a secret."

*Boris promised, "Not me, I never will tell anyone."*
*"Cross your heart and hope to die?" asked Igor.*
*"Cross my heart and hope to die!" announced Boris.*

The two brothers slept in late the next morning. Boris went to the well to get some water and met a neighbor. "Why are you so late today?" asked the neighbor and shook his head with a "tsk, tsk, tsk."

"Don't ask me. Just don't ask," replied Boris. "We were up late last night walking in the woods and field."

"Why were you doing that?" inquired the neighbor.

Immediately Boris whispered to him, "To get the pot of gold my brother found and buried in the field. That's why. But don't tell anyone—it is a secret."

It wasn't too much longer after that when the whole village was talking about the pot of gold. By that very evening the news reached the master's ears. The master immediately sent his servant to bring Igor and Boris to him.

A short time later, when Igor and Boris were before the master, he shouted at them angrily, "How dare you think you can keep the news of the treasure of a pot of gold from me? How dare you!"

Igor answered, "What treasure, sir?"

With a red face and veins popping up in his neck, the master screamed, "Don't lie to me. I know all about it. Now the truth. I know you found a pot of gold because your own brother told one of the neighbors about it."

"My brother Boris?" asked Igor. "You know him. That silly fellow is always full of silly tales."

"We shall see about that," cried the master. He faced Boris and demanded, "Did Igor find a pot of gold?"

"Yes, sir, indeed he did," said Boris. "Please lord, don't tell anybody. It is a secret."

"So! You went at night to get it," demanded the lord.

"Yes, we did. We did," answered Boris.

"Now we are getting somewhere. Tell me all about it. Right now!" commanded the master.

Boris shuffled his feet, looked down at the floor, and then at the master. "Well, first we walked through the orchard and there were bagels growing on the trees."

The master interrupted him, "What bagels?"

"The ones that must have rained down from the bagel cloud," said Boris.

"M-m-m-m-m," said the master as he stroked his beard.

Boris continued, "Then we found a fish in the fox trap. After that we found a fox in the fishnet. It was a water fox. Then Igor went to the spot in the field and dug up the pot of gold."

"What happened after that?" asked the master.

"That was when we went home," said Boris. "We had to go past your house and it was when the devil was whipping you. We clearly heard your cries."

"You are crazy!" roared the master.

"Oh no, sir. Don't you remember? You were squealing like a pig." Boris replied and bowed to the master.

"What a miserable story. Give that fellow a good beating and throw him out! In fact, give his brother a beating as well. That will repay them for wasting my time!" ordered the master. "Get those fools out of here!"

Boris moaned and groaned as he limped on his way home. On the other hand, Igor was grinning as he walked. He was well pleased with himself because he knew they could live in peace and plenty for the rest of their days. From that day forth, Igor always had a special affection for every bagel he ate.

*An adaptation of an old Russian tale.*

# *Nasruddin's Donkey*

(Persia)

Nasruddin went to the market place and put up a sign, "Someone has stolen my donkey. Whoever stole it, if they return it I'll give it to them."

When asked why he would do this, he said, "There are two pleasures in life to find something you have lost and to give away something you love."

# *Why the Bear's Tail Is Like It Is*

(Norway)

It was a clear, cold, winter day near winter solstice, and Bear and Fox met in the forest. Fox had come along the trail dragging a string of fish he had stolen on the snow.

Bear saw him at once, saw the fish, and figured that something was going on.

"Hi Fox," greeted Bear. "That's quite a string of good looking fish that you are dragging behind you."

Fox got a crafty look in his eyes, "Thank you Great Bear. I have been out fishing and caught these fish up in the stream where there is a good pool loaded with them," oozed Fox.

Well, the Bear enjoyed a good fish dinner, and he was good at wading out into the waters and catching fish. He thought that might be a good way to spend the afternoon, so he asked the Fox how he caught them.

The Fox narrowed his eyes, "I know that you know how to catch fish. You get out onto the ice, make a hole and stick your tail down into it. Of course, you must keep it there as long as you can. Don't be bothered if your tail feels something biting on it. That's the fish, of course. The longer you keep your tail dangling in the water, the more fish you will get. Then when you judge it to be time, give your tail a good cross-pull sideways, make sure it is a strong pull. You will see what happens."

Bear thought that this sounded like a good idea and an easy way to catch fish so he followed Fox's directions. He went back to the stream where he knew the pool of water was. He went out on the ice, dug himself a good size hole, turned around and sat on it with his tail dangling in the water. He sat like that for quite some time until he decided that it was time to give his tail a strong cross pull and lift out the fish. So he pulled his tail out, with a strong cross-pull and, well, it snapped off short.

And so, dear ones, that is why Bear has a short stumpy tail to this very day.

# *The Hunter's Bargain with the Devil*

(Finland)

There was this fellow with a family. A very large family. He and his good wife had 16 children. They lived off of what he was able to hunt. What they didn't need to eat, they sold, and with the money they got they bought what they needed. Then, one fall, the man had a lot of bad luck hunting. He would get some game, but very little, and some days he would get none at all. The poor fellow was afraid that he had lost his luck.

One day when he was out hunting in vain, a man suddenly appeared beside him in the woods. He was wondering who this man might be since he hadn't seen him come or heard him walking. There was something strange about this fellow. The stranger said, "Hello hunter. What are you thinking?"

"I wasn't thinking anything. I guess maybe I was just wondering why my hunting luck has been so bad. I was only thinking to myself." said the hunter.

"I'll make a bargain with you," the stranger said. "For three years you can go to the island in the swamp. You will have to do nothing else but sit there and shoot and I will drive the game there to you. But after three years, you must shoot for me a bird that I have never seen before. If you are not able to shoot such a bird, then we will talk further. Is it agreed?" asked the stranger.

The hunter thought for a while but he really didn't have a choice. So he agreed to it. The stranger took a piece of paper out of his pocket.

"A mark must be made on the tree, some blood from your little finger must be dripped on the paper and then our bargain is made."

They made the contract and the man disappeared, but the hunter noticed that where he had stood were hoof marks, not the footprints of a man. Now he knew why he was so uneasy about the stranger; and he also knew that he had just made a bargain with the devil. There was nothing else he could do about it now so he went to the island in the bog. He got several loads of birds and as much forest game as he could handle.

It was like that every time he went to the island. For three years he killed as much game as he could. He sold most of it and became rich. When the three years were just about up, he became nervous. His good wife noticed he was suddenly impatient with the children and fretted about little things.

So she asked him, "What has happened to you? Why are you so upset? Isn't life good to us? What trouble do you have?"

Since there was only three days left until the end of the three years he decided he wouldn't keep it a secret any longer. He told his wife of his agreement with the devil and explained that there was no way he could shoot a bird that the devil wouldn't recognize since he probably knew them all.

"What will happen to me? What will I do now?" he whispered to her.

The hunter's wife thought for a while and then said, "Here's a bird that he doesn't know. Before you have to go to the island on the third morning, tar me all over and I will get into the feather basket and turn myself around well, and then you will see a bird that no one has ever seen before." This woman was clever because after all, as a mother of 16 children, she had to be!

So, on the third morning, she was well tarred. She was tarred front and back and all over. Her husband was amazed when she went to the feather basket and turned herself around there. It was impossible to consider what she was. Everyplace on her was covered with feathers.

They went to the forest in the middle of the island and the wife told her husband, "You stay here and I will go over to that grassy spot. When the devil comes and asks you, tell him you have already shot a bird he has never seen before. Bring him over to me. He will surely not recognize what kind of bird I am."

The hunter did as she said. As he was sitting there, the stranger suddenly appeared again in front of him. "It has been a good three years for you hasn't it? Are you ready to finish the bargain we made? Are you ready to go with me now ?" he asked.

The hunter replied, "But the bargain was that if I shot a bird you did not recognize I will have finished my part of the pact. I shot such a bird just this morning."

"Where is this bird?" asked the stranger with a puzzled look.

"Over there on the grassy area. Come see," said the hunter as he led the stranger over to the spot. "There it is. Have you ever seen such a bird?"

The devil looked at it, examined it and walked around it. "Surely I must know what kind of a bird this is. Let's see,-no, it isn't that. Well, I once knew, no, that isn't it. How have you managed to kill such a big bird? How were you able to find a bird I never saw before? A-ha, you have shot it with two bullets. It seems that one has gone straight and the other has just made a flesh mark."

"Yes, that is exactly the way I did it," mused the hunter.

The devil stamped his hoofs and stomped around. "I guess you have won the bargain. Since you did, for three more years I will drive the game your way. Since you were so ingenious as to kill a bird that I have never seen, you have won."

After the devil left, the hunter and his clever wife went home. They had quite a job to get her clean again. In fact, it was necessary to heat the water in the tub several times and scrub her. She finally did come clean though. After all, wouldn't a woman who had 16 children know all there is to know about getting clean?

For three years, the hunter brought game from the same place and they finally had enough money to last them for the rest of their lives. The hunter prided himself on his very clever wife and she spent many happy years with him. Somewhere, the devil is probably still looking for another bird like the one he had never seen before.

# *Coyote and Fox*

(United States)

Coyote was out in an open field, chasing a field mouse from clumps of brush to rocks to tall grasses, but he could not catch him. Coyote skittered around to make sharp turns when the mouse executed a quick change of direction. Fox, watching all of this from a distance, shouted "Ooo-oo-ooo-hoo!" Of course, Coyote found this taunting upsetting and he became very angry; stopped his chase of the mouse and instead took out after Fox.

Fox was prepared for this and led Coyote on a frustrating hunt. Coyote was startled to find Fox standing by a fire when he caught up with him. Now, Fox had started the fire, but what was surprising was Fox started to plead with Coyote not to eat him.

"Please don't eat me. We are both in danger from the fire. The only way we can save ourselves is to climb into two burlap bags that are nearby."

"Why should I do such a thing?" asked Coyote.

Fox, however, soon convinced Coyote that they must hurry and save themselves.

"Quick Coyote, get into this sack and I will tie you up and then I will get into the other one and tie the bag up myself. I know how to do this. Hurry! We must save ourselves."

Coyote was convinced by the urgency of Fox's actions, and he agreed. Fox threw one of the burlap bags over Coyote and being wily Fox, threw the sack into the fire and ran away laughing. Coyote managed to get out, but not before he was painfully burned. Now he was really mad, "Just you wait Fox. I'm going to get you and you will be my supper!"

Coyote followed Fox's trail and found Fox holding up a huge boulder. "The rock is about to fall on us," panted Fox. "I am getting really tired of holding it up. I need to go get a drink from the lake. You hold it while I am gone so it doesn't fall on us."

Before he really thought about it, Coyote put his paws on the boulder and pushed, waiting for Fox to return. The longer he held it, the angrier he got until Coyote decided he really didn't care if the rock fell or not. He let go of the rock and of course, it didn't fall. Coyote was furious and took off to find Fox vowing to make Fox suffer before he became his succulent supper.

Coyote loped off to the lake and found Fox. He was just about to pounce on Fox when Fox told him to wait.

"I'm sorry Coyote. I have been trying to get the cheese in the water to bring to you," said Fox. Fox pointed to the reflection of the moon in the still water of the lake.

Coyote, was quite hungry by this time. "Climb on the log," Fox told him, "and I will push it near the cheese so you can get it." Coyote did as Fox ordered and as soon as Coyote reached the end of the log, Fox tipped it over and "splash!" Coyote fell into the lake. If there is one thing that Coyote hates it is being in water, but worse than that is being tricked by Fox again.

When Coyote got to the shore, he didn't even take time to shake the water from his hide. Beside himself with fury, he took off after Fox. He dug his paw-nails into the ground, once again determined to do horrible things to Fox. Coyote found Fox quietly stirring a stick inside a beehive. Fox was very careful about the way he stirred.

"What are you doing now?" demanded Coyote.

"Sh! I am teaching school, can't you hear my students reading?" answered Fox. "I am being paid a dozen fat hens for this. Do you want to teach for a while? Since I have sported with you I'll make it up to you. You teach for a while and I will go get the fat hens and share them with you."

Greedy Coyote forgot his rage. All he could think of at this moment was how hungry he was. He could hear the reading inside the beehive, so he felt safe.

"All right, I'll teach them," and Coyote started stirring the beehive with the stick. He was very cautious with his stirring at first and then he got bored and gave the beehive a whack and the bees boiled out of the hive and stung him everywhere. They stung him so badly that he could hardly see. Half blind, hurting everywhere and in such a state of hostility Coyote kicked up clouds of dust as he tore after Fox.

Coyote found Fox calmly sitting and eating a watermelon. "I am eating half of this watermelon. That was so it won't be so heavy to carry the other half to you," explained Fox.

"Of course I was going to bring your share to you but since you are here now, why don't you eat your half Coyote?" Fox sounded so sincere. "In fact Coyote, I'll get another watermelon tomorrow if you will get us another one the next night."

The watermelon patch belonged to an old couple. When they discovered some watermelon missing, they set up a scarecrow covered with tar. The next night when Fox came, Fox found the scarecrow and said to it, "Do you think I am afraid of you?" Fox struck the scarecrow with his left paw and then when he couldn't get away, Fox kicked at the scarecrow with his hind feet. Fox was completely stuck.

The old couple found Fox stuck to the scarecrow and were about to kill him. "Don't kill me," pleaded the Fox. "Coyote has been forcing me to steal. If you let me go and let me take a melon to Coyote, I'll get him to come to your watermelon patch himself tomorrow night." The Fox seemed so frightened of Coyote that the old couple agreed.

Fox returned to Coyote with the melon and bragged as he told Coyote all about the scarecrow. "It caught me but it was easy to get loose. You won't have any trouble with it tomorrow night."

Coyote went to the patch the next night and found himself the prisoner of the scarecrow covered with tar. He smacked the scarecrow to show how cool he was. When he got stuck, he smacked it with his other paw. He couldn't get any of his paws loose and his tail was even plastered tight into the tar. The old couple grabbed Coyote and strung him up on a tree and skinned him. They left only the hide with his fur on top of Coyote's head and on his paws. "Never come back here again," they warned Coyote and they let him go.

Coyote decided that he would never again have anything to do with Fox. Fox had gotten him into so much trouble, he was done with Fox forever. Fox was nearby and watched Coyote trotting away.

Fox started to laugh, "Goodbye Coyote! You look so much better than when I first met you. Look at your handsome toupee and furry gloves." Coyote just kept on walking, wiser but certainly a different looking animal than when he first started to chase Fox.

*This story comes from the San Luis Valley in Colorado.*

# *The Fly, Moth, and Mosquito Challenge Anansi*

(Africa)

One hot, hot day on the plains of Africa, a fly, moth, and mosquito were out hunting. They happened upon Anansi the spider who was out strolling in the tall grass. These three flying hunters signaled to one another, "Let's get Anansi," and they swooped down on him. "What a tasty meal he will be," whined the mosquito.

The problem, though, was that all three together were not able to conquer him. On the other hand, Anansi was not able to beat them, so they struggled. After quite a long struggle, all four of them were exhausted and no one was a winner.

"Why did you attack me?" asked Anansi.

The fly, moth, and mosquito, sitting on a plant leaf answered, "We were hungry. We were all out hunting, and because all living creatures must eat, we intended to eat you."

"Well, you were not able to beat me, and so you will never be able to eat me. Why should I not eat you three?" gasped Anansi.

"Ha! You were not able to get the best of us. How could you eat us?" they asked in a chorus.

"I have an idea," Anansi said with a chuckle. "Why don't we have a lying contest, and the winner gets to eat the loser." The three flying friends agreed.

Anansi decided to establish the rules for the contest: "Here is how we will do it. Each of us will tell an outrageous story. If I tell you that your stories are lies, you can eat me. If you tell me my story is a lie, I get to eat you."

The moth started his story first. "One day four days before I was born, my father was clearing new ground for a garden with his sharp bush knife. He cut his foot with the knife and had to be carried to his bed. Well, I got up finished clearing the ground, plowed, planted, and tended the seed and harvested the crop. Four days later when I was born, my father was already a rich man."

Anansi curled himself up into a ball and thought about the moth's story. The fly, moth, and mosquito giggled as they waited for his answer. Finally, Anansi said, "How true. How true. How amazingly true." Now the three friends were surprised. They did not expect Anansi to give that answer, so they were forced to continue the contest.

Mosquito flitted around until he found the perfect place on the leaf to settle down and tell his story. "One time when I was hunting," he said, "I killed and ate an elephant. After such a big meal, I lay down in a clearing to play with the elephant's ear. A leopard came walking by, and because I was no longer hungry, I decided to play with the leopard. I chased him, caught him, grabbed him by the neck, shoved my fine fist down his throat, grabbed his tail from the inside, and pulled him inside out. The leopard had just eaten a sheep, and now the sheep was on the outside and the leopard was on the inside. The grateful sheep thanked me and went off munching and grazing into the grass."

Anansi untangled his legs, stretched, pondered, and said: "How true. How true. How amazingly true." Once more the three friends did not expect Anansi to give this answer. In fact, fly, moth, and mosquito were startled with Anansi's answer. And so, fly told his story.

"There I was out hunting, and I saw a fat antelope. I slowly raised my gun, took aim, squeezed the trigger, and shot at the antelope. Then I ran forward, caught the antelope by the neck, killed it, and skinned and quartered it, and then my bullet came flying by. I caught the bullet and replaced it in my gun. Because I was quite hungry after all of this excitement and wanted to eat my catch alone, I climbed a tree with the meat, built a fire, cooked the meat, and ate it all. When I was finished, I was so full that I could not climb down from the tree. Do you know that I had to go home to my village, get a rope, come back, and tie it to a limb of the tree to let myself down?"

Anansi turned himself around in several circles, cleaned all of his legs, and finally said, "How true. How true. How amazingly true." Again the three flying creatures did not know what to make of Anansi's answer. So now it was the time for Anansi to take his turn in the contest.

"One day I was walking through the forest when I came upon a coconut lying in the path," said Anansi. "I picked up the coconut and called out to see if anyone could hear. 'I have just found a coconut,' I shouted. 'If no one comes to claim it, it is mine.' No one claimed it, so I took it home, planted, watered, and tended it. It grew. At last when it was a mature coconut tree with coconuts of its own, I climbed the tree and cut down three ripe coconuts. Then I cut each coconut open with my bush knife. When I cut open the first coconut, a fly flew out. When I cut open the second one, a moth fluttered out. When I cut open the third coconut, a mosquito buzzed out. Because the coconut belonged to me, the tree that grew from the coconut belonged to me. And because the tree belonged to me, the coconuts that grew on the tree belonged to me. And because the coconuts that grew on the tree belonged to me, the contents of the coconuts also belonged to me. So the fly, the moth, and the mosquito belonged to me. Because they belonged to me, I could do with them whatever I pleased. And I pleased to eat them. However, when I tried to eat them, they ran away. I have been looking for them ever since. And at last here they are, my fly, my moth, and my mosquito."

Fly, moth and mosquito were speechless. They each wanted to say, "How true," but they couldn't because that would admit that they were Anansi's property. Then it would naturally follow that he would eat the three of them. They couldn't say, "That is a lie!," because they would then lose the contest, and Anansi would eat them. They took the only possible course of action. They ran off into the forest. And that is why, to this very day, when spiders go hunting, they hunt for flies, moths, and mosquitoes. And when they catch them, they eat them, crunch, crunch, crunch. And the reason is that flies, moths, and mosquitoes belong to spiders because spider won the liar's contest. "How true. How true. How amazingly true!"

# Happy New Year
(China)

*The lunar calendar changes after 12 months of 29.5 days, on the eve of the second new moon after winter. This is typically between January 21 and February 19. Approximately every 2½ years a month is added giving the calendar a Lunar Leap Year. This calendar system also involved a 60-year cycle that contains five cycles of 12 years in which each year is named for an animal. Each person born in each animal's year, it is believed, would carry some of their attributes. So, Happy New Year to the Chinese who believe that the year of a person's birth is the primary factor in determining that person's personality traits, physical and mental attributes and degree of success and happiness throughout his lifetime.*

*Whenever you happen to go to a Chinese restaurant, notice the placemats. Many times they have the creatures that the years are named for as well as some character traits exhibited by these animals. You can figure out what creature was associated with the year you were born.*

Over five thousand years ago, the Jade Emperor of Heaven decided to call all of the animals in the kingdom to a Feast. He was aware that the calendar was based on the seasons of the year, when to plant crops and when to harvest them. No one knew when they were born, therefore, there were no birthdays to celebrate. There were no special events and times to recognize them and again, as a community celebrate them. Life just went on from day to day with no history or memories of the past. The Jade Emperor of Heaven's plan was to establish a calendar where these important times could be featured.

He sent out invitations to the Feast so that the animals could establish a time to greet each other, wish others good health, long life, and happiness, and enjoy memories of the past. On the appointed day, only twelve animals arrived. Let us now find out which animals they were and what the Jade Emperor of Heaven decided to do.

When the invitations arrived, the conditions were that the animals were to race through the thickest part of the forest, swim across the river at its widest point, and the Emperor would honor those who arrived.

Cat and Rat lived together in those days in peace. They were friends and shared food and happenings together. While eating a meal, Rat asked Cat to think about how they would be the first ones to arrive at the Emperor's Feast. "Racing through the forest shouldn't be too hard. Difficult, but not impossible," said the Cat.

Rat thought for a while and said, "Let's see if Ox plans to be part of the race. He is so big and strong he could push through rough places and even the widest part of the river should be no problem for him. He might agree to take us with him."

"That's a good idea," agreed Cat. "We could ride on his back and from our perspective, we could direct him for the best part of the jungle to travel through."

After their repast, they wrapped up several food morsels to take to Ox and find out if he was interested. Ox considered their thoughts about the race and grunted, "It would be of interest to me to take part in the race. It also would be quite nice to have you as travel companions. I agree."

So the three of them made their plans. When the time came to begin the race, they were surprised that many of the creatures they knew weren't going to take part. The race was to begin in some meadows and then go from there to the forest. Cat and Rat climbed onto Ox's back and decided where they would best be able to travel in comfort. Cat went to the broad back of Ox where it would be easy to reach out and grab Ox's tail for balance. Rat decided to sit on Ox's head so the view would be clear.

Ox rushed off with the other animals when the race began. The meadow was covered in a hurry. Then came the outer forest leading into the thickest part of it. Ox had no trouble clearing a way. Rat had to duck sometimes to avoid branches and vines. Cat was quite secure with the tail for help.

Even though Cat and Rat had played together, slept together and shared all their meals, Rat was thinking about how he could trick Cat and Ox and win the race himself. The easiest way he thought of was to wait until they were in the river and trick Cat into losing the tail grip. In the forest, Rat grabbed a vine that was part of the plan to dislodge Cat later.

They saw other creatures having a hard, slow time traveling through the forest and the river stopped many of them from being part of the race. Some animals just reached the end of their desire to race so they gave up on it.

Rat could see from his vantage position that Ox was leading all the others in the race. Tricky Rat planned to slide off of Ox when they got out of the water and take advantage of Ox slowing down to enjoy a drink and slog through the mud on the banks of the river.

While they were still out in the river, Rat took the vine and wrapped it around Cat's legs, gave it a tug and dragged Cat off of Ox and into the river. Cat looked astonished and tried to overcome his dislike of water. Cat was not a good swimmer and Rat could see Cat looked mangy and bedraggled from struggling in the water.

Rat also noticed that other animals were being swept downstream because they were not strong enough swimmers to avoid being carried away. Just before Ox climbed up on the shore, Rat jumped off, cleared the mud and weeds and scampered away. Meanwhile, just as Rat knew, Ox drank water and became mired in the mud by his weight. Rat scampered just as fast as possible and was the first animal to reach the Jade Emperor of Heaven, who announced, "Rat, you have won the race. You are number one."

By this time Ox lumbered into the gathering spot and was given the number two place. The third animal was the Tiger. The fourth animal was a very tired Rabbit. The fifth animal was Dragon who flew in to the finish line. Amazingly, Snake had managed to cross the river on a log and slithered in sixth. Horse galloped in and slid to a stop for seventh place. Next to arrive was Sheep, for the eighth place. Monkey, who had swung through the forest lost speed in the river and came in ninth.

Rat hadn't observed Cock during the race and was surprised to see Cock come in tenth. The eleventh animal to come to the finish line was Dog. And the Boar came in twelfth place.

Then limping through to the finish line was a most wretched-looking Cat. Cat was not only wretched looking, but mad from the treachery of Rat. The Jade Emperor of Heaven sympathized with Cat.

"You have not been a winner in the race but you persevered and made it where many other creatures gave up and quit."

So the Emperor and all the winners enjoyed the Feast which consisted of jellyfish, crab meat, shark's fin soup, sea cucumber with black mushrooms, crispy chicken, steak kew with broccoli, bird's nest seafood, duck with eight stuffings, steamed fish, fried rice, chicken lo-mein and fruit.

The prize for the winning animals was announced by the emperor. "One of the twelve years will be named after each of you, with the order of the years established beginning with Rat followed by subsequent winners."

Cat and Rat were never friends after that and that explains why Cat tries to capture Rat and wreak revenge for Rat's trickery.

# *Tall Tales*

*If you wish your children to think deep thoughts, to know the holiest emotions, take them to the woods and hills, and give them the freedom of the meadows. The hills purify those who walk upon them.*

*Richard Jeffries (Nature essayist, 1848–1887)*

# *Febold Feboldson*

(Great Plains, United States)

This legendary Swedish pioneer, Febold Feboldson, was a hero on the Great Plains. Back in the early days, he was the best drought-buster there ever was. No drought dared to come out of Kansas because, Febold Feboldson would have that darn thing busted within 24 hours.

What kind of a person would you expect such a drought-buster to be? Mean and ornery? Nasty? Well, Febold Feboldson was certainly not of that ilk. He was the best-natured fellow that anyone could ever know. In fact, folks declared that they had never seen him all fussed-up about anything.

That was until the year the weather got hotter and hotter, drier and drier and a full-blown drought was in full-bloom. That drought spoiled Febold's fishing. There he sat at his favorite fishing spot, which had dried up. "Well now, this sort of situation needs to come to an end," he muttered to himself. He sat down on a pile of dusty dirt and began to ponder about what he should do.

One thing that Febold was, was a fast thinker and on this particular depressing day, he pondered and came up with over a hundred possible ways to bust this drought that had doomed his favorite fishing hole.

Now, even today, if you were to travel north to the North hills, there were many lakes. Even those lakes had suffered from the dry times but there was still enough water there for the folks who settled around the area. During a drought, they would be forced to go to the lake area, find a nice fresh-looking lake and wade down into it and cover themselves with the cool, refreshing water to keep themselves from drying up and blowing away. They actually had to do this several times a day!

Febold decided to solve the problem. He gathered brush, wood and dry branches and built huge bonfires around these lakes. He was kept busy feeding fuel to the flames to keep them going for three weeks. Well, it was still hot, hot, hot and in those three weeks, the water in the lakes got so warm that it just vaporized and turned into fluffy clouds.

There were so many of these clouds that they bumped into each other trying to float away from the lakes, which created torrential rains in the area. It seemed as if, once primed, the rains came again and that saved the country. You would think that this would make Febold famous and certainly of heroic proportions. But, not so, because the new problem was, that without the lakes, the Indians had no place to swim.

Being versatile, this clever Swede discovered the "noise method" to make rain. It was a highly satisfactory method. How did he discover this? Well, he recalled that it generally rained after noisy battles, national political conventions, horse races and a favorite past time of seeing if a man could outrun a horse in a race. That's when people's cheering and shouting created quite a noisy event.

So, to make enough noise, he had to think of how to overcome people who were too lazy to cooperate. These white settlers proved to be so lazy that they couldn't speak, let alone shout and yell. Just like I told you before, Febold wasn't a person to accept being stumped. Especially when he wanted to go fishing as badly as he did.

He decided to encourage his fishing companions—the frogs—to help him. These frogs had good loud croaking voices. But there was just another problem. Febold recognized that a frog, any frog, will not croak unless he is good and wet. Then, he croaks!

It didn't take Febold too long to overcome that problem. He hypnotized several frogs by telling them, "It is raining. Isn't that wonderful! I feel so much cooler already."

As he kept bragging about how cool and wet it was, the frogs began to croak with bliss and joy and spread the froggy good news to other frogs. Why, it wasn't too much longer before every frog in the country was croaking and puffing itself up to give some mighty croaks.

It was only a few minutes of this noise before the local Indian rain god got a great headache. Then just as Febold knew it would, there was enough noise to bring on a real downpour of rain. You could see the drops splashing in the dust and settling down to create wet, dark spots. Everyone was happy, especially Febold, the settlers and the frogs. That was only one of the ways

Febold created rain for the parched Plains and its occupants. The Plains that had been in a terrible drought were now gushing with water. He found that he could only use this solution to the problem once a season, but so much rain fell that the frogs were washed clear down to the Gulf of Mexico. That gave Febold a whole year before those frogs were able to get back. By that time, Febold had already invented and discovered several other possible ways to bust droughts!

# *Jim Bridger in Yellowstone*

(Wyoming, United States)

Jim Bridger found it hard to communicate to friends and acquaintances about the marvels he was discovering in his rambles in Yellowstone. As one of the first explorers there, he saw many amazing sights that defied description.

People that he corresponded with began to doubt his word. Some came right out and said, "What a liar!"

Others just scratched their heads and wondered what had happened to their friend. There were those who suspected that he must have fallen and hit his head with a horrific whack.

For instance, there was the time, he said, that he was riding up a narrow ridge and came to the end of the land with only a gorge ahead and sheer cliffs on either side.

Now the problem became obvious to Jim when his horse wouldn't stop, no matter how hard he pulled on the reigns and shouted, "Whoa! Whoa! Whoa, dern you, whoa." The blamed animal just kept picking his way forward confidently stepping right off the cliff.

Miraculously, they didn't fall to their certain deaths but walked straight across to the next ridge. How was this possible? Jim remembered that this was the haunted place in the Yellowstone, where even gravity was petrified. Yes, there were many people who questioned the state of Jim Bridger's mind when he passed on some of his stories and experiences.

# *Squirrel Meets His Match*

(Colorado, United States)

One lovely summer day I was enjoying a hike along a section of the Colorado River where some rocks rose from the middle of the stream. As I came around a corner in the trail, I saw an extremely agitated squirrel scampering and scooting back and forth along the bank. I stood motionless and watched him for a while, then looked at the river to see what had attracted him.

There on top of a big boulder was a peanut. That was it! The squirrel wanted that nut! Suddenly, the squirrel changed his route and scampered away from the river; then turned around, dug in his feet furiously, and raced back to the river. He took a mighty leap and darned if he didn't land on top of the rock! I was so happy with his success, but decided to stay and watch because I wanted to see how he was planning to get off the rock.

He sat out there in the sun with his tail curled around him and carefully broke the peanut open and took out the nuts. He stuffed them into the sides of his mouth (I could see the bulges in his cheeks); then he explored his rock. It was a good-sized rock, but nothing special.

I could see that he was now trying to figure out how to get back to the bank. He finally attempted a short field take-off, but I could see he wasn't going to make it. I was prepared to watch him get dunked.

Then a big greenback cutthroat trout flashed out of the water and snatched the squirrel in mid-air. As I stood there stunned, I was even more stunned to see that greenback cutthroat trout's head come out of the water again and carefully place a peanut on the rock.

# *Old Red*

(United States)

Old Red was one amazing hunting dog. He was so clever, he counted birds and would even give a bark for each bird. One of the pompous men in town was skeptical about the dog's owner boasting about Old Red's ability to count. He was in a deep argument over who had the best hunting dog and his couldn't count, but he sure could hunt and howl.

Old Red was such a good bird dog that he would flush the birds out one at a time so that the hunter could take his time shooting them. Again, the envious townsman doubted this until he saw Old Red in action; he grabbed his gun and crashed through the bush to see how Old Red did it. He found that Old Red had herded the birds into a rabbit hole and had covered the entrance with his paw. Old Red then released the birds one at a time.

Later that day, Old Red ran by while shaking a sassafras bush with a knot on the end. That dog looked like a crazy dog as he kept hitting the townsfolk with the bush. The skeptical fellow, thinking the dog had gone mad, took out his gun and shot Old Red. The furious owner of Old Red stormed up and roared, "Shoot, he was only trying to tell us that there were more birds than you could shake a stick at, out on the lake!"

# *Old Blue*

(United States)

Old Blue was the best coon and possum hound dog in all the state. All Old Blue's owner had to do was to show the hound a board and Old Blue would go off and find a possum or coon whose hide would fit the board. Old Blue's owner never had to worry about finding a board to fit a hide and he never needed to worry about the quality of the possum or coon skin.

Old Blue disappeared one time for three days. His owner went out in the woods to see if he could find any trace of his clever hound. He searched for hours and then just as he was about to quit looking, he found Old Blue. The dog was resting beside an oak tree stump and was worn out and exhausted, so Old Blue's owner carried him home cradled in his arms.

Old Blue's owner wondered what had happened to the dog for a long time, and he finally figured it out. Just like in the cartoons, a light bulb suddenly went on in his brain! He saw what the problem was one day when he went out on the back porch and saw his wife's ironing board leaning against the porch. Old Blue must have seen it and gone out in the woods and wore himself to a frazzle trying to find a possum or coon with a hide big enough to fit that ironing board.

# *Dead Dog*

(United States)

Down home, there was this fellow who had a wonderful rabbit dog. That dog was the best dog the fellow had ever had, and he had some good dogs before. Then the dog up and died. The grieving fellow decided that he had to do something special to remember the dog, so he skinned him and had his wife make a pair of gloves out of the dog's hide. He used those gloves regularly and it always made him think of his good old rabbit dog.

The fellow was out in the forest working one day and he pulled his gloves off and laid them down on an oak stump. He sat down on another oak tree stump to eat his lunch. Just as he was biting into his sandwich he saw a rabbit run out of the underbrush and before his astonished eyes, the two gloves jumped off of the stump, grabbed the rabbit as it went by and choked it to death.

# *Brownlee Goes Bear Hunting*

(Colorado, United States)

It seems a bear had gotten into a horse corral in Eldorado so I went to Denver and bought a heavy-duty bear trap. The trap was attached to a chain and a treble hook which would drag, enabling someone to follow the bear until the hook grabbed something.

I baited the trap with burnt honey on a stick hanging from a tree. The next day the trap was gone and when they found it up the Fourth of July Creek, there were only two toes in it.

The next summer, I got a radio call that someone had seen Three Toes up around Diamond Lake so I got my shotgun and took off up the trail. Soon I saw a bunch of people coming down the trail and they were scared.

I saw the bear around the edge of the lake and shot at him. Now, when you wound a bear, it makes him mad. That's when he started after me. If you have ever been on the Diamond Lake trail, you know it is anything but a highway. I went so fast that the trees began to look like a board fence as I ran by. I was really moving and got tired, so I climbed a tree. I knew the bear was crippled but when he got to the tree I was in, he came right up. I jumped to the next tree and went down and he came right after me. So I went up the tree again. We kept that up until the bark was so smooth it was hard to climb.

Then Three Toes got some wood in his feet and slowed up so I went on ahead to the mine dump. I only had one shell left so I put it in my gun. Then I put in a bolt and a nail and just when the bear got between me and a stump, I let him have it. The nail went right through his tail and stuck him to the stump and I went over and hit him in the head with a two-by-four until I killed him.

And if you don't believe it, here's one of his feet. And those are the bear facts!

# *The Frogs and the Norther*

(Oklahoma, United States)

It was in the fall of 1888, or thereabouts, when ol' man Tim Montgomery, was livin' just to the outside of Tulsa. He lived where there were some horse stables, but they aren't there today. Things do change, except the weather. He lived in a broken down cabin an' hit's gone now of course. There was a big ol' frog pond nearby that was full of frogs that were plunkers n' chunkers n' clunkers, peepers n' cheepers n' bleepers, moaners n' groaners, boomers, squeakers, ronkers n' blonkers' n' thumpers, n' they all sang, sometimes alone n' sometimes together, they liked music!

Back in those days, hit was just Tim n' that pond n' AAAWWWLLLL them frogs, n' that's where this story begins.

Seems like ol' Tim didn't git much schoolin'. That didn't mean he was dumb or nothin'. Just means that back in them days folks didn't have many schools to go to, nor the time and opportunity to go them, neither. But, even without schoolin', ol' Tim was a mighty smart man. Tim was specially smart about tellin' the weather. Now, he wasn't no meteorologist or nothin' like that, he jist had lived abouts in that same country for a lifetime, n' a lifetime of livin' kin teach a lot to folks that wants to learn. Now, ol' Tim had watched the regular goin's and comin's of the hail and the sleet and the snow and the ice and the chinooks and the winds and the sunshine and the rains, that he had jist got mighty good at readin' all the signs an' perdicktin' the weather. He had a reputation that wouldn't quit for bein' accurate about the weather.

Now Tim's specialty fer perdictin' weather was perdictin' the comins' and goins' of Northers. A norther's a storm that hangs around in the country fer most of the winter, off n' on. A norther's a divil of a storm too. Hit comes on fast. Hit don's give ye much time to think an' move out of the way. N' when hit comes, hit lays everythin' flat. Blows up outta the north country, long with black, boilin' clouds, n' claps of thunder n' lightnin'. Then the wind howls down, layin' the grass flat out, n' bendin' trees half over. Then, come the ice, the snow, n' the cold. Happens fast. Happens REAL fast. People in these parts know what I'm talkin' 'bout.

Tim somehow always knew when a norther was on the way. Knew it fore' ennybody else knew it. He could look at the sky n' study the clouds, n' test the air n' watch the way the grass laid over. Tim could jist smell a norther comin'.

Well, now, one lazy day the end of the fall season, all the harvestin' done n' all the stock safe away in the barn, ol' Tim was settin' in his ol' rockin' chair up on the porch of the cabin, jist a lookin' out over that frog pond that was there at the bottom of the hill.

The air was warm n' most of the sky clear, but for a blackness growin' up in the north. Tim rocked n' rocked, n' watched up there along the northern skyline. The wind picked up. It shifted round to the north. Sky got darker, clouds boiled up a bit n' the grass began to rustle ever so little. Ol' Tim looked up at the north sky, got up out of the chair and sauntered on down to that frog pond. Got to the pond n' clumbed up on a big rock down long that pond. Sat up there, looked up at that north sky, watched the clouds boil up higher n' blacker, watched the grass lay down partway, heard the thunder n' saw the lightnin'. Tested the wind with his finger, gettin' colder. Then ol' Tim leaned out over that frog pond n' began to whistle up a little tune for them frogs.

He whistled a frog song he jist happened to think of. N' all them little frogs there in that frog pond, now they liked music, and they listened. Then they all stuck their little heads up out of the water, and all of them little frogs, they answered Tim's whistle. An' all of them little frogs swam a little closer to that rock n' they waited.

Ol' Tim, sittin' up there on that rock, looked up at that north sky, watched the clouds boil up higher and thicker and blacker, watched the grass lay down flatter, listened to the thunder, saw the lightnin', and tested the whistlin' wind with his finger, gettin' colder. Then ol' Tim leaned out over that frog pond agin' n' began to whistle up another little tune fer them frogs. Tim whistled the first part of a new song n' all them little frogs in that frog pond, now they liked music, n' they listened. Then they all stuck their little heads up above the water, n', all them little frogs, they whistled back Tim's song. An' all of them little frogs swam closer to that rock, n' they waited.

Ol' Tim, sittin' up there on that rock, looked up at that northern sky, watched them clouds boilin' up higher n' higher n' gittin' thicker n' thicker, n' blacker n' blacker, watched the grass lay down flatter n' flatter n' flatter, listened to that rollin' thunder buildin' louder n' louder, n' saw that silver lightnin' flashin' closer n' closer, and stuck his finger up into that whistlin' wind to test it, gettin' mighty cold. Then ol' Tim leaned out over that frog pond a third time n' whistled them frogs another little tune. He whistled the first half of a third song. N' all them little frogs in that frog pond, now they liked music, n' they listened. Then they all stuck their little heads up out of that water, n' all them little frogs, they whistled back. N' all of them frogs swam closer to that rock n' they waited.

Ol' Tim, sitting up there on that rock, looked up at that northern sky, watched them big, black, boilin' clouds roll in overhead, watched that grass lay all but flat over, sat still under that roaring thunder n' that crackin' silver lightnin' all round, and poked his finger up into the roarin' wind to test it, gettin' mighty cold. Then ol' Tim leaned out over that frog pond agin', fer the fourth time, n' whistled them frogs another little tune. He whistled n' all them little frogs in that frog pond, now remember, they liked music, n' they listened. Then they all stuck their little heads up out of that water, n' all them little frogs they whistled back. N' all them frogs swam closer to that rock n' they waited.

Ol' Tim, sitting up there on that rock, looked all round. That storm was ever' where now. His clothes n' hair whipped out in ever' direction. Little bits of corn snow n' ice began to pelt through the air. N' the clouds boiled low down n' dangerous-like, black n' dark n' fearsome as ever clouds can be, n' that grass was laying down flat as ever it could be, n' the thunder was ever' where n' that lightnin' struck all round ever' where too.

One more time ol' Tim poked his finger up into that wind to test hit, n' that wind near tore his shirt sleeve off, too. What with his hair n' clothes a-blowin' like that, n' that fist a pokin' up into the sky like that, darned if ol' Tim didn't look like one o' them ol' timey prophets you hear tell about. Well, n' hit was cold almost to freezin' too, n' temperture ready fer the bottom to drop out. Ol' Tim leaned out over that frog pond jist one last time, whistled up one last tune fer all them little frogs. He whistled a beginnin' to a fifth tune. N' all them little frogs in that frog pond, now they liked music, n' they listened. Then they all stuck their little heads up out of that water, n' all them little frogs, they whistled back. N' all them little frogs jist swam up to that rock n' climbed up out of that water n' sat right there, all of 'em, thousands of 'em right there round the bottom of ol' Tim's rock, while that norther howled all round. N' all them little frogs, they waited.

Now ol' Tim watched the sky. Sat still waitin' in them clouds that roared n' boiled all round. Sat still n' waited while the thunder boomed n' the lightnin' pounded down n' the snow came in great gustin' sheets. Saw how the grass was crushed flat n' felt how the wind ripped at his clothes n' tore at his hair. Poked that forefinger up into the air one more time to test the wind. Hit was cold like the innerds of a meat locker with the tempeture fallin' fast. Ol' Tim leaned out over them frogs ever so slow, then spread his arms n' opened his hands . . . n' then . . . WHOOOMMMMMPPPP!!!!! He clapped his hands together n' all them little frogs leaped up off the ground, high into the air, all thousands of 'em, n' back down to the water in the pond, all together they did. N' just as all them little frogs hit the water, jist as their little heads n' arms was into the water n' all their little legs was still up in the air, that norther hit fer serious. Tempeture hit rock bottom. Jist in that very second, that frog pond froze solid flat clean over. There were all them little frog legs stickin' up in the air jist like that!

Didn't I tell ye that ol' Tim was no dummy, fer not havin' much schoolin'? Picked himself up offin that rock, walked back up to the barn, got himself a scythe n' came on back down to that pond. Scraped all them little frog legs off the ice, jist like that, thousands n' thousands of 'em, double. Packed 'em all in ice and straw to keep 'em, n' sold 'em all to a place up in Chicago. Took three trains cars to haul 'em all away. Made himself some money, nuff to save n' nuff for a good time besides.

# *Kansas Weather*

(Kansas, United States)

We lived out in the plains of Kansas during the summer of the big tornado. I mean the BIG tornado. Early that summer, lightning had struck a big, black kettle that sat on our back porch and turned it inside out! That kettle stayed that way until the big tornado came back and turned it right side out again. That same tornado blew in through a window of our house. It changed all of the rooms around and even put in an extra bathroom on the first floor. Then it went out as quickly as it had come.

Further on down the road, that same tornado blew all the feathers off my neighbor's prize chickens and put them on a young pig. That neighbor of mine had the coldest looking chickens and the funniest looking pig you ever did see! Later that same day, his cow's tail was blown right through the trunk of a tree. He had to saw the tree down to free that darn cow. Then for a glorious finish, another bolt of lightning struck the huge haystack out in his field. It burst into flames like the largest candle you ever did see from a distance.

Yes, indeedy. I haven't seen things like that since I left Kansas.

# *Dog Days*
## (Nebraska, United States)

*A friend of mine, Roger Welsch, a farmer and folklorist in Nebraska tells the following story.*

"When the real dog days come to Nebraska it really gets hot. I don't think there is any place hotter. In fact, farmers feed their chickens cracked ice so they won't lay hard boiled eggs. It gets so hot that the river dries up and the catfish have to come up to the house to get a drink at the pump.

One hot day last summer, it got so hot in the middle of corn season that corn started to pop. A herd of cows was grazing next to the cornfield and they saw all of that popcorn floating down and they thought it was snow and every one of those idiot cows stood there and froze to death! That's what a hot day is like.

A day or two later it got so hot that I took a hamburger patty out of the freezer, tossed it up into the air, and when it came down it was cooked, well done. But I had to be careful and not toss it too high. You have to toss them just right or they can burn if it is too high. That's hot.

That same summer my neighbor had to prime himself before he could spit. But it got hotter and dryer and that neighbor's wife had to run their well through a wringer to get enough water to cook with.

That summer, the river got so low and stayed that way that the frogs grew up to be three and four years old without ever having learned how to swim. Then there was the time one farmer was out plowing and it started to rain. The first drops that hit him shocked him so much that he passed out. To bring him to, they had to throw two buckets full of dust in his face. Don't ask me about hot!"

# *How Cold Was It?*

(Maine, United States)

It got so cold that sounds wouldn't even travel outside. If anybody said anything, you had to grab a few words out of the air and take them inside to thaw out by the fire to tell what people said. Once it got so cold that one fellow told us about icicles that trapped telephone talk. One day when a call did not go through, they calculated the location of the freeze-up, sent an engineer to the thirty-third telephone pole beyond the bridge, and broke off the seventh icicle south of that pole. The engineer took the icicle into a warm café, held a tape recorder next to the icicle, and captured the conversation as it thawed.

It was so danged cold that on the side of the road was a pair of beagle dogs that had a pair of jumper cables on a rabbit to try to get him started.

# *The Winds of Texas*

(Texas, United States)

Whenever you happen to travel in Texas, you might want to question people about the winds. Scientists have listed Texas as the top state for natural disasters. Certainly, the following information might give the listener some reason to pause for thought when driving in Texas.

No matter where you go in Texas, you hear about a weather phenomenon they refer to as "crowbar" holes. The holes are created when the winds get to blowing really strong.

If the bars bend, the wind is normal. If the bars break, it is not safe to go outside. This gives a whole new meaning to the term "wind sock."

# *Family Stories, Local Legends, Hoaxes, and Urban Myths*

*A miner is a liar who owns a hole in the ground*

*Mark Twain*

# *It Was a Dark and Stormy Afternoon*

(Pennsylvania, United States)

*This story is one I heard from my father during the depression years. We had a family farm in western Pennsylvania and life there was that of another time. We heated the house by way of a pot-bellied stove in the front room that burned coal dug from an exposed seam near the spring.*

*Facilities included the traditional little house at the end of a path. And according to tradition, there was a crescent moon carved in the door of it.*

*There was a natural gas pipeline to the house, and we had gas lights in every room. It goes without saying that this was a time before television or radio. Our amusement consisted of family music-making and storytelling. The front porch swing was the stage for the telling.*

*Dad first told me this story when I had managed to get into trouble with my mouthing off. I have added details to the story that appear in this version.*

Dad and I were walking the farm lane from the barn, over to the turnoff, to the lane that went down the hill through the oak grove to the farmhouse. It was a cold and blustery fall day with dark clouds and swirling winds blowing the leaves from the trees. Great huge snowflakes began to fall.

Overhead we saw a dark cloud of birds heading for warmer climates. As we watched, we noticed one small bird near the end of the other birds was losing altitude and slowing down. It came to earth on the lane above the barn and just sat there. We could see that it was shaking with cold.

The family plow horse ambled from the barn. The snow fell in a wet, heavy blizzard and soon blanketed the lane and of course, the snow covered the bird. "Well kid, let's go help that little guy," my dad said.

Just as we started to do that, the farm horse came alongside the quaking little bird. To our shock, the horse "dumped" right on top of the bird covering it completely. Dad never missed a chance to laugh at events that tickled him. I joined him in his laughter. "Now kid, we have a mess," he chuckled.

We could see the steam rising from the fresh horse "dump" and to our surprise, we heard tentative bird sounds coming from within. The little bird was rejoicing in its newfound warmth. Its birdsong took on a sound of joy.

Then dad pointed to the barn and sitting there was the farm cat. We encouraged the cat to reside there since it kept the rodent population under control. The cat sat there confused. Its head swiveled, listening. It located the source of the bird song it heard and the cat began to stalk the sound. It came up to the lane and stood over the "dump." The cat cocked its head as it listened.

Dad was laughing with a belly-laugh now. "This is something to watch," he said. And so, we watched. Before our surprised eyes, the cat lifted its paw and swiped the top off the "dump" and snatched the bird out of its cozy hiding place. It was all quite swift and the cat ate its prey, cleaned its whiskers and headed with a contented swagger back to the barn.

"Well, kid. There you see it all. Sometimes it isn't our enemies that 'dump' on us, and sometimes it isn't our friends that rescue us. But for sure," dad said as his green eyes danced, "sometimes it pays to keep your mouth shut!"

# *Sometimes It Does Take a Rocket Scientist*

(United States)

*Humor assumes many sources. You can find stories such as the following on the internet or they can be found in souvenir programs, where I found the original version of this one. The souvenir program was part of the Longs Peak Scottish/Irish Highland Festival held at Estes Park, Colorado from September 5-8, 2002. This publication contains a schedule of events and locations, tributes to people and musical groups performing, advertising, plus articles of interest including folklore information and ethnic stories. Here then, is my retelling of one of the stories.*

A Scottish scientist who worked for NASA built a gun specifically to launch dead chickens at the windshields of airliners, military jets and the space shuttle, all traveling at maximum velocity. The idea was to simulate the frequent incidents of collision with airborne fowl to test the strength of the windshields.

British engineers heard about the gun and were eager to test it on the windshields of their new high speed trains. Arrangements were made and a gun was sent to the British engineers. When the gun was fired, the engineers stood shocked as the chicken hurled out of the barrel, crashed into the shatterproof shield, smashed it to smithereens, blasted through the control console, snapped the engineer's backrest in two and embedded itself in the back wall of the cabin, like an arrow shot from a bow.

The horrified Brits sent NASA the disastrous results of the experiment along with the designs of the windshield and begged the Scottish/NASA scientist for suggestions.

NASA responded with a one-line memo: "Thaw the chicken first."

Several features in this story contribute to the humor, and deserve comment. First of all, the Scots have produced many groundbreaking scientists. Recently, for example, the cloning of Dolly, the sheep came to the world by way of Scotland.

Another aspect of the humor in this story is the existing rivalry between Scotland and England. It is similar to jokes about North Dakota as told by Montana citizens. Humor comes with many layers providing the laugh or smile.

# *Fur-Bearing Trout*
(Colorado, United States)

The state Fish and Game Commission has issued a special license to fish for these wonderful creatures. Gift shops sell pictures of fur-bearing trout to fortunate visitors. Local taxidermists have trout in muskrat coats available.

How did these amazing, unique critters come to be? Blame it on a drummer back in the old days; an old, isolated miner who was peddling a medicine-show remedy, and cure-all line of merchandise. He was carrying his load in a backpack when he came to a bridge over a stream.

The dew of the morning was fresh on the wooden logs of the bridge and the drummer took an unexpected slip and slide. He fell and some of his wares broke loose and it was in this way that he spilled two jugs of powerful hair tonic into the stream near Leadville. All of his profits became diluted in the rushing, tumbling water and went on its way downstream.

Shortly after this accident, bearded fish appeared, and could only be caught if the fisherperson had a rod painted like a barber pole.

This is a year-round sport, since fur-bearing trout can also be caught in mid-winter if you use snow worms as bait. Picture a remote shoreline filled with barbershop decorated poles. It was a sight to behold any season of the year, and the shouts of joy as the successful fisherperson dragged one of these furry fish ashore were triumphant. Imagine the envy of the patient fishing folk who had never ever caught one of these prizes. Now, there is some grist for real fish stories. Have you heard any of them lately?

# *The Sheep That Was Quite Different*

(Colorado, United States)

When I first came to Gothic, Colorado, in the late eighties, it was a humdinger of a town. The mines were working and shipping ore. The hills were full of prospectors. We had a post office, stores, a good hotel, a church and seven salons.

The Single Jack Saloon was owned and run by John McAvoy. Not long after I arrived in Gothic, McAvoy, on his way home from Marble, was caught in a snow slide in Crystal River canyon. The coroner found his body the next July. I was picked to take charge of and settle the affairs of the Single Jack. And that is how I got myself into the saloon business and got to know a beer-drinking mountain sheep.

Most of McAvoy's trade seemed to stay with me. Among them was young Bill White. Bill only took a drink now and then, but he liked to come over in the evenings and yarn about big game hunting. The royal sport was hunting Rocky Mountain sheep. A fine pair of horns of a mature ram was the grand prize.

One morning about the middle of May that year, I met Bill riding one horse and leading another. He was out of fresh meat. He said that he had heard that there was a band of mountain sheep near Maroon Pass. He was going up to see if they had found the right kind of pasture as he wanted them to be in good condition when the hunting season opened.

"Good idea," I replied, "but what are you doing with that rifle?"

"Oh," Bill grinned, "the rifle is for my protection in case I meet a bear."

That night I was alone in the Single Jack and heard someone at the back door. There was Bill, a sheep's carcass tied on one of his horses. He was on the other horse with something wrapped up in his slicker. He dismounted with the bundle, came slowly into the saloon and laid his burden on one of the tables. I could see that he was worn, tired and unusually serious.

He explained what had happened. As he neared Maroon Pass, he sighted a band of about sixteen sheep led by a large ram with a magnificent pair of horns. The ram saw Bill and gave a signal to his charges. At the next glance, the sheep had all vanished. All of them, except a fine young ewe, which stood looking at him from a patch of quaking aspen.

Bill sighed, "I sure thought that ewe was loco but I got her with an easy shot. When I reached where she was lyin', I found a little lamb snuggled against her dead body. The lamb was only an hour or so old and too weak to run. So, as sheep will do, the mother had licked that little feller all over and ruffed up his hair and then fed him. That's why he was still alive."

Bill's troubled face was streaked with dust and sweat as he turned to me and added, "Judd, I ain't no angel. Generally I'm tougher than I ought to be, but I just couldn't leave that pore little feller there to freeze and starve after I'd killed his mother while she was trying to save him. So, to make a sad story short, I brought him along with me. I can't take care of him, but Judd, you can keep him here in your saloon, and old-timer, you have just got to do this for me." Bill reached for the bundle and unwrapped it before me.

There was the poor little feller shivering and starving. The lamb moved his head and let out a low, plaintive, "Ba-a-a." That settled it.

"I'll do the best I can for the kid," I answered.

We made a bed for the newcomer in back of the stove. Then I went over to Charley Howe's hotel and told them of the addition to my family. I got them to give me a bottle, on which, after considerable scurrying around, they managed to fit a nipple.

It was remarkable how fast that lamb grew and developed. The children liked to play with him, but before long he became too rough. In a short time his horns began to show. Some small dogs tried to play with and worry him, but after some bumps from his hard and knotty little head, they left him alone.

The boys at the saloon had great sport with my pet sheep. He was in and out of the Single Jack much of the time. A few years before this, President U. S. Grant had passed through Colorado. The little sheep strutted around as if he were commander-in-chief of the whole works in Gothic, so the boys began to call him "General Grant." This name stuck, but was usually shortened to "General."

The General soon graduated from the milk bottle and nibbled at grass, leaves, shrubs and alfalfa. For a change of diet he would go over to the hotel, and even one or more of the cabins, to make selections from the garbage pails.

Growing bolder, he would slip into the hotel dining room, and if no one was there, he would reach up on the tables, knock over the sugar bowls and lap up the sugar.

As the General grew older, he enlarged his zone of activities. If he found a miner's cabin empty, he would go in and raise the very devil. His favorite pastime was to climb into the middle of a bed and jump up and down until the springs squeaked in agony. Sometimes, like a spoiled youngster, he would become so delighted with the sport that he would overstay the time for his visit and leave the bedclothing in a very bad state indeed.

That night an irate miner would call on me at the Single Jack and make the lights blink in relating what he thought of the acts, doings, character, ancestors and final destiny of that cussed sheep of mine. The only thing I could do was to send for the whiner's bedclothes and have them washed. Before long, I was doing the washing for almost every old sourdough in the camp.

The costs of taking care of my vexatious pet became so burdensome that I began to think I must get rid of him, when a fortunate discovery came to my relief.

The General jumped up on a table where I was working. He was in my way and to get him to move, I gave one of his legs a sharp slap. To my surprise, he bounded into the air, sailed over and alighted like a leaf on another table ten or twelve feet away. The length of that jump was just plumb amazing. I was sure that few people would believe that any animal could jump that far from a standing start. It seemed to me that in a town like Gothic, there would be many who would bet the General could not make such a leap. Here was a chance to have the General make back some of the money I had spent and was spending, on him.

That ram was a bounding, jumping machine. When he lit from a bound, he could either stick there or make a marvelous second bounding leap. Having made a happy landing, he would stand there proudly to show what a great jumper he was.

After a number of trials, I found that his limit was about fifteen feet. But if you, yourself, will set two tables that far apart, you will see that a jump from one to the other would be quite a feat.

From the start, the General's public jumping was quite a success. My customers greatly enjoyed the sport, in fact I began to make more money on that ornery sheep than I did on selling liquids from the bar.

One day, when we had quite a crowd, in walked the General in his usual swaggering manner. One of the boys said, "Here comes the General. He's been making money for us. I think we ought to give him a treat"

"Sure," another said, "but what can we give a sheep?"

Someone yelled, "How about a glass of beer?"

The bartender drew a glass of beer and set it on the bar. The sheep sniffed at it, and then let it alone. Someone shouted, "That glass is not big enough. It ought to be one he can get his nose down into." So the barkeeper filled the biggest glass he could find. Still the sheep would not drink.

"I saw him lickin' salt scraps over at the hotel. Put a handful of salt in the beer," the man said.

That was done.

Then, marvelous to behold, the General put his nose down into that beer and drank it all up. The crowd roared. I was playing a game of pinochle in another corner of the room. I threw down my hand and went over to see what all the noise was about. The men excitedly told me what the sheep had done. One said, "Give the General another one. Show the boss what his pet will do. Forget the salt this time."

The sheep looked at me with his bright amber eyes and solemnly finished off this glass also. "That's enough," I ordered.

The next night I called some of the boys together at the Single Jack and told them, "Fellows, I want you to have a good time here, but I think we should cut out giving any more beer to the General. After those two big drinks you could see that he was wobbly. If we keep that up, it will spoil his jumping. None of us would want that, would we? Anyway, drinking will make him a worse pest than he is now." They reluctantly agreed. But when I was out of the way, some troublemakers would slip the General one just so they could see him drink.

If a stranger came in and ordered whisky, wine or some such drink, nothing unusual would happen. But if he ordered beer, the stranger might be startled to see, standing with his forefeet on the bar, a large handsome Big Horn sheep, with his bright golden-brown eyes fixed on the glass of beer, clearly indicating that he would like a little of it. Some men would be frightened, but most of them would laugh and then order the General a glass of beer just to see what he would do with it. By this time, the General had so progressed in his newly acquired accomplishment that he would drink the beer with perfect decorum.

One of the increasing numbers of onlookers was sure to order the General another beer. This he would accept and drink in the same courtly manner. Then, having reached his limit, he bade them adieu.

Not long after the beer-drinking development, I was confronted one day by Charley Howe. I realized that my pet had been up to some new depredation. Charley did not go into details but looked at me sourly and said, "Judd, I have stood all I can from that blasted sheep. I'll give you just three days to get rid of him, and if you don't do it I will."

When I reached the saloon, I found a well-dressed, heavy-set stranger waiting for me. He greeted me cordially. He spoke excellent English, but with a German accent. He tried to tell me his name, but I could not pronounce it, much less remember it. So I said, "If it is all right with you, I'll just call you Herman."

"Sure," he replied, "dat vill make me feel at home." Herman said he was looking for manganese properties.

Just then General Grant walked in with his usual lofty manner. Herman was at once interested in the sheep and asked many questions. My guest was treated in a display of some expert jumping, but of course, not on wagers.

That evening my friend found himself in congenial company. There were metal miners and prospectors. Among them were engineers, assayers, foremen and superintendents. Herman ordered beer. Just then, Herman felt a tug at his elbow and turning, saw the General standing beside him with his forefeet resting upon the bar. The ram was not only standing beside him, but also was plainly indicating that he wished to join Herman in the amber fluid he was drinking.

"Bartender," said Herman, "Serve dis handsome sheep your tallest glass of beer, and let's see vat he does mit it." The General drank sedately and expertly, knocking his glass bottom up, evidently to show Herman that he found the beer good to the last drop. Herman was surprised and delighted. He exclaimed, "Look at der sheep drink beer. He iss der chum for me. Mr. Judd, I vant to buy der sheep and take him back to Germany mit me."

I could see that Herman, even though he was a little high, was serious about wanting to buy the General. So I called him aside to talk business. It did not take us long to come to a satisfactory agreement.

The boys now realized that their pet was to be taken away where they would never see him again. It was comical to see them crowd around the General and bid him goodbye.

About noon the next day, Herman and I were standing in front of the Single Jack preparing to take leave of each other. The German then told me he was an officer of the Governmental Zoological Gardens in Berlin. He said the board of trustees of the zoo had sent him to America to procure specimens of wildlife to add to their collection. In particular, they wanted a fine young male bighorn Rocky Mountain sheep to be used in experiments in crossbreeding with mountain sheep of Europe and Asia.

Herman admitted that while he was in Denver he had heard about the jumping sheep and had made a special trip over to take a look at him. He was delighted with his find, but had not disclosed whom he represented for fear he would have to pay too high a price for the animal.

"Well, Herman," I answered, "it was not such a bad deal on my part, for that very day Charley Howe had told me that if I did not get rid of that blasted pest in three days he would make mutton out of the sheep and feed him to the hotel guests."

Just then, up drove the teamster with a fine pair of horses drawing a well-cared-for ore wagon. He lifted his right hand, palm down in the old-time Colorado salute.

The teamster was my old friend Bill White. With unusual soberness, Bill looked at me and said, "Well, Judd, you did a swell job in taking care of our little Rocky Mountain lamb. If there is a sheep heaven, I am sure the mother sheep will look down and smile."

*This story was given to the author by an old Cornish miner, Jack Owens, a member of the Clear Creek Metal and Mining Association.*

# *Yellowstone Park Grizzly Bear*

(Wyoming, United States)

A few years back, The National Park Service changed its tradition of dealing with bears in Yellowstone National Park. It used to be that the bears lined the roads and were treated as cute little teddy bears by park visitors. This writer has personally seen grown adults place small children beside roadside bear beggars, and step back to take pictures of their offspring and the bears. This is not a tall tale—we saw people doing this regularly. Of course the population of small children diminished somewhat from such events each season, but parents still ignored the warnings and continued the practice.

At any rate, the Park Service decided to close all garbage pits, which used to serve as the gourmet cafeteria for bears, and remove the bears from the parts of the park where tourists congregated.

The grizzly bear is on our endangered animal list today, and the griz specifically, was targeted for relocation. Still today, scientists argue loud and long as to what the garbage and relocation policy has done to the griz population. In fact, I am sure this policy is just one step toward the extinction of this amazing beast. I was engaged in heated discussion with one of my Yellowstone Park Ranger friends about this matter and the gauntlet was tossed "show me a grizzly bear in Yellowstone Park and I will eat it!" Rash words, but heartfelt.

So, my friend George and I set out for a several day backpack into the backcountry in search of a bear. He assured me that we would find one. One of the things you first think of when going into bear territory is survival. This includes wearing bells that will jangle as you walk. One of the things you most want to avoid is surprising a bear, especially one with cubs, especially if you get between the mother bear and her cub! George also encouraged regular, even loud, talking and singing. This was also to let the bear know someone was coming.

Another precaution was some see-a-bear-training. The instructions were detailed. If we were to come upon a bear and were in a dangerous position, DO NOT RUN. I repeat, (as George did), DO NOT RUN. Drop to the ground, curl yourself up into a ball, protect your head with your hands and arms and remain motionless. That was the key course of action. DO NOT RUN. The reason being, that a bear can easily outrun a person.

So, we took off and for the first afternoon we talked, sang, and jangled. That evening we camped by a delightful lake. We were very careful with our foodstuff so that we wouldn't attract bears. We hung our supplies and cooking pots from branches in the trees after cleaning them carefully. Early the next morning we ate, cleaned up camp and once more started our bear stroll. Late on this second day, I was more confident than ever that we would not see any bears and I started talking in a normal conversational voice. And then it happened. It was the worst—we surprised a bear! George, beside me, dropped to the ground in a curled ball with his hands and arms protecting his head.

Instinct for survival was too strong in me—I ran and started scratching my way up the nearest pine tree. Yes, I know bears can climb trees, but as I said, the survival instinct was strong. From the branches of the tree, I looked down and saw the bear pawing the George-ball. The bear swatted George with his paw several times, walked around him sniffing and George remained motionless and soundless. I climbed up a bit further; and that was my undoing because the bear heard me.

The bear left George-ball and lumbered over to my tree. It looked up and then with its huge paws with opposable claws, started climbing. I skinned my body in my effort to get higher but the bear was gaining altitude on me. Then I felt his claw tearing at my boot. The next thing I felt was his claw pulling at my leg, just as I am pulling yours!

# The Miners' Refuge

(Rocky Mountains, United States)

When the miners worked in the Rocky Mountain area, the first thing they had to do for the mining community, was dig a hole of good depth in the ground and build a little necessary building to fit over it. This was called "The Outhouse."

The mining camps had running water—the streams near them. Other than that, no modern plumbing or luxuries. Now, the outhouse in the mining camp that Mike and his partner Sean worked in, had a rather unique feature. When you opened the door of it, which usually had a crescent moon carved in it, you saw the plank across the hole had two large oval holes cut into it. That meant that using it was a sociable situation.

After lunch one day, Mike and Sean both needed to use the facilities, so there they were in the outhouse. Mike was still seated when Sean go up and prepared to hoist his trousers up but a quarter and a dime fell out of his pocket and rolled over to the empty oval and dropped straight down into the hole. Mike sat there and laughed at Sean's loss.

Quietly, Sean finished hoisting his trousers, and buckled his belt. He stood there and looked down into the hole. He spotted the quarter and dime down there. He pulled at his chin a bit and then put his hand into his pocket and took out some change. He pondered a while and chose another dime. He threw it down into the hole.

Well, Mike stopped laughing when he saw this. Sean looked into the hole and then carefully took his wallet out of the back pocket of his pants. He opened it and looked inside. He slowly took out a dollar bill, put his wallet back in his pocket, leaned over the oval hole and watched his dollar float down into what was below.

Mike was astonished, "Now, what on earth was that all about?" A dollar was a lot of money back in those days, and Sean was tight-fisted with his money.

Sean looked at Mike with indignation "Well, you don't think that I'd go down there for 45 cents, do you?"

# *Prunes*

## (Colorado, United States)

*The town of Fairplay, Colorado, is the county seat of Park County and is located eighteen miles from the geographic center of Colorado. And how did this town get its name, you ask? Of course there is a story behind that.*

Mr. William B. Webster says his grandfather, William Wilcox Webster of Summit County named the town in 1879. Mr. Webster was going to a meeting with a fellow miner who had made a strike of rich ore. It was a proverbial dark and stormy night, and Mr. Webster was stopped on the trail by a horseman coming from the opposite direction. While talking with the horseman, Mr. Webster noticed a bullet hole in the crown of the man's hat. Even though he was curious, he knew that it would be wise to refrain from asking too many questions, especially of a stranger.

Later that night, Mr. Webster came upon a tent city on the trail. One tent was larger than the others. When he went inside he found four men playing cards and having an agitated discussion. It seemed they had just finished burying a man that had been killed in a duel. A stranger had entered their tent and accused one of the card players of murdering his sister two years before, and said he allowed that he had been looking for him ever since. He challenged one of the card players to a duel in front of the tent.

Both men fired their pistols, and the miner's bullet struck the crown of the stranger's hat while the stranger's bullet killed the miner.

Webster realized that the man he had met on the trail had been part of the gunfight. Webster asked if this tent town had a name and the men replied that it did not, Webster said, "Let's call it Fair Play!" And so the name of the place was two words until October 1, 1924 when the Postal Service mandated that Fairplay was officially one word.

Fast forward to The Great Depression. A saloon owner with a flair for promoting figured out a way he and his regular customers could make Fairplay a tourist attraction. Big Dan Riordan came up with a grandiose scheme in May of 1930 to make Fairplay the "Burro Capital of the World." He announced that they would need to erect a monument on the main street of the town to the jackass, the workhorse of the local mines.

Someone said, "That's a good idea but we need a dead burro to bury in the monument."

Riordan remembered that there was the dead body of one up on the Alma dump at the present moment. Someone said, "It needs a name—let's call the burro 'Old Prunes'." Everyone got a good laugh out of it but the planning took on reality.

"How about a story going that the Hoffman brothers, Louis and August, were takin' care of him, but he got so old he couldn't eat, so they put 'im out of his misery?" mused one of the fellows.

"That's good," gloated Riordan. "Prunes it is. We will create a monument that the whole country will talk about and dedicate it to the memory of that most admirable of beasts—our beloved old friend, Prunes."

The idea worked. In fact the entire country did come to know the story of Prunes. Thousands of Colorado school children grew up speaking his name. As is usually the case, other cities vied for the honor of Prunes being theirs.

In fact, Prunes was a very ordinary burro. He had spent a year or two in the old Hock Hocking mine, tramming ore from the underground. Later, he had worked in other pack trains in the district. When the mines began to close, he had been turned loose to fend for himself. In fact, he became a community pet, living off handouts from area housewives and children. Later, when he grew old and feeble, lost all his teeth and showed signs that his days were numbered, the Hoffman brothers shot him and carted his body to the dump. According to everyone's best estimates, the burro was about 22 years old.

Riordan decided that fact wouldn't be part of this great memorial to a burro. He announced that Prunes had been part of the mines in the 1860s. The story included his role in many of the important local mines, and he was now part of the area's history.

A sculptor was commissioned to come up with a suitable monument. Another irony to the grand story—it wasn't until the unveiling that everyone discovered the artist didn't know much about burros. Instead of depicting the hard-working leader of a jack train, he sculpted a pregnant jenny. Just a little bit of a difference!

So far, Fairplay had a nice (if inaccurate) monument. The inscription to the monument stated "PRUNES, A BURRO, 1867–1930, FAIRPLAY, ALMA, ALL MINES IN THIS DISTRICT." The creators of this hoax ignored the fact that the oldest age for a horse which is a blood cousin to the burro, is just 62. Didn't the monument give Prunes' age as 63? Wonder of wonders!

The whole hoax took off when a local character who looked like an old hard-rock prospector, Rupert E. (Rube) Sherwood claimed that Prunes was his beloved burro. Never mind that Rube was given to spinning tall tales over a wee taste of whisky and who hung around the lobby of the hotel smoking his smelly pipe. No one contradicted him.

Shortly after the monument was erected Rube announced that he had bought the animal for $10.00 in 1879 and that he and Prunes had roamed throughout the gold fields of Colorado. "Prunes was the greatest and most loyal friend I have ever had."

Rube asked that his own remains should be cremated after he died, and placed alongside those of his faithful old companion. Riordan and his cohorts now had the best of all stories—a love story. Almost immediately newspapers throughout the Rocky Mountain region picked up this touching story. Pictures of the monument were printed everywhere. Included in many of these pictures was Rube standing mournfully beside the statue.

Editorials appeared. The city of Denver even wanted to dig up Prunes' bones and transfer them in the city. In the midst of all of this, Rube produced a poem about the burro, titled "Me and Prunes."

*My old Burro pard "Prunes" has cashed in, it's kinda bad, but in a way,*
*Mebbe it's better th'ol'boy has eased off an' is callin' it a day.*
*I'm a goin' to miss him scandalous—it just can't ever seem th' same,*
*Not a havin' him a standin' here an' not a hee-hawin' in the game.*
*Together, we sure drawed cards a-plenty, just ol' Prunes and me.*
*We bucked th' play, no matter how th' cards was dealt you see,*
*Sometimes we filled our hands an' won, but so seldom it was a joke.*
*Most times endin' with a bob-tail flush—an' windin' up stony broke.*

Along with five other verses, this poem left scarcely a dry eye. The full poem is encased under glass in the memorial. Rube died on August 23, 1931 in Fairplay and the burial ceremony before the monument was attended by politicians, military brass and representatives of most of the area's press.

Old Rube's ashes, in a bronze urn, were tucked into their final resting place just as Rube had requested.

As stories have a habit of doing, it seemed to grow with more small details added here and there. For instance, one story claimed that Prunes once saved the lives of a group of miners who were snowbound high in the mountains. All alone, Prunes fought the raging wind and the deep drifts and made it to Fairplay with a grocery list tied to his halter. The grocer filled the order, strapped it on the burro's back and Prunes fought his way up the mountain again just as the starving miners had given up all hope.

Another story told of Prunes saving Rube's life in a mine where the two of them were working. Prunes sensed an impending cave-in and threw his body against his beloved master, forcing him backward into the clear just as the whole mountain gave way and filled the mine with rubble.

There were also those who bragged that Prunes could read the labels on cans. Somehow, there were several witnesses who were perfectly willing to swear to this fact.

Big Dan Riordan never really succeeded in resurrecting the fortunes of Fairplay. The town did manage to grow, but then the population withered away. History books are published with this story in it. Occasionally, newspapers print articles and photographs of this bit of lore to entice people

Here is the Prunes Memorial in Fairplay, Colorado. Observe the pregnant jenny carved in stone at the top of the monument. Pregnant jenny? Also, how old? Prunes was an "old timer" according to these figures. Photograph by Norma J. Livo

to travel to Fairplay and view it for themselves. One thing remains—the monument to Prunes and his beloved Rupe. Even today, as you drive by the main street statue and memorial, you might see awestruck tourists reading the inscription and poem. Others may be photographing this momentous bit of history. It all proves that a good story lives on and on and on.

# *Killer Rodents on the Rampage*

(Colorado, United States)

The vast number of rats inhabiting the rocky crevices and cavernous passages at the summit of Pikes Peak has recently become formidable and dangerous. These animals are known to feed upon a saccharine gum that percolates through the pores of the rocks apparently upheaved by some volcanic action.

Since the establishment of the government signal station on the summit of the peak, at an altitude of nearly 15,000 feet, these animals have acquired a voracious appetite for raw and uncooked meat, the scent of which seems to impart a ferocity rivaling the fierceness of the starved Siberian wolf.

The most singular trait in the character of these animals is they are never to be seen in the daytime. When the moon pours down her queenly light they may be seen in countless numbers trooping around among the rocky boulders that crown the barren waste, and during the warm summer months they may be seen swimming and sporting in the waters of the lake, a short distance below the peak, and on a dark, cloudy night, their trail in the water is marked by a sparkling light, giving the lake a bright and silvery appearance.

It had been a few days since Mr. John T. O'Keefe, one of the government operators at the signal station upon the peak, returned to his post, bringing with him a quarter of beef upon a pack animal. It being late in the afternoon, his colleague, Mr. Hobbs, immediately left with the pack animal for the Springs. Soon after dark, while Mr. O'Keefe was engaged with shuffling through paperwork in his office, he was startled by a scream from Mrs. O'Keefe, who had retired for the night in an adjoining bedroom, and who came rushing into the office screaming: "The rats! The rats! We are under attack! Help!"

Indeed there were thousands of vicious vermin invading through windows and doors and cracks in the building.

Mr. O'Keefe immediately encircled his wife with a scroll of zinc plating, such as is used in roofing, which prevented the savage creatures from climbing upon her person, and although his own body and limbs were being covered with them, he succeeded in encasing his legs each in a joint of stovepipe, and then with a heavy war club, preserved at the station with other Indian weapons captured at the battle of Sand Creek, began a desperate struggle for the preservation of his life.

Hundreds of animals were killed on every side by the rapid and well-aimed blows of the murderous bludgeon, yet still they seemed to swarm in with increasing numbers from the adjoining room, the door of which had, by a fatal oversight, been left open. The entire quarter of beef was devoured in less than five minutes, but it seemed only to sharpen their appetites for still fiercer attacks upon Mr. O'Keefe, whose hands, face, and neck were already terribly lacerated.

In the midst of the warfare, Mrs. O'Keefe managed to reach a coil of electric wire hanging near the battery, and being a mountain girl familiar with the throwing of the lariat, she hurled it through the air, causing it to encircle her husband, making innumerable spiral waves along which she poured the electric fluid from the heavily charged battery with all the fullness of its power.

In an instant the room was ablaze with light, and whenever the rats came in contact with the wire they were hurled through the air to an almost instant death.

The sudden appearance of daylight, made such by the coruscations of the heavily charged wire, caused the ravenous creatures to abandon their attack and take refuge in the crevices and caverns of the mountain, making their exit by way of the bedroom window through which they had forced their entrance.

The saddest part of this night adventure upon the peak is the destroying of their infant child, which Mrs. O'Keefe thought she had made secure by a heavy covering of clothing. But the rats had found their way to the infant (only two months old), and left nothing of it but the peeled and naked skull.

Doctors Horn and Anderson have just returned from the peak. It was thought at first that the left arm of Sergeant O'Keefe would have to he amputated, but they now believe it can be saved.

******

What a tragic story! What hardships the people of 1876 had to endure! What a hoax! Readers are more eager to believe a good story than the boring, dry truth. After this shocking story, O'Keefe restrained himself until late 1880 when he once more created chaos. One of these subsequent stories was about his trusty mule Balaam and a massive herd of deer and later an attack by ravenous mountain lions. O'Keefe also invented a story about volcanic activity rumbling on Pikes Peak.

In 1875 John Thomas O'Keefe was appointed the chief of the corps' signal service station atop Pikes Peak in what was then the Colorado territory. His job was to record the daily events of the weather on the mountain such as rainfalls and snowfalls, barometer and temperature changes, wind velocities and other natural phenomena that played over the peak.

O'Keefe soon found that this was no exciting assignment, but a rather boring job on the lonely mountain, isolated among the clouds much of the time. He seldom had any visitors except during the summer months and his supply trips to Colorado Springs were his only other contact with people. Other than that, his telegraph key was his only contact with the outside world.

Becoming bored, he drew upon his naturally vivid Irish imagination and sense of humor. He became a storyteller, creating his own mountain world filled with imaginary creatures and experiences. Some of his stories came off the mountains with hikers who had visited with him. Other stories O'Keefe told to friends and fellow employees of the U.S. Army Signal Corps.

Of course friends and fellow workers were familiar with his wild, humorous fabrications, but there were others who believed.

Scientists scoffed at the horrendous tale. They put forth the fact that rodents did not live above timberline. Others stated that O'Keefe wasn't married, let alone the father of a two months old daughter. He earned the title of "The Pikes Peak Prevaricator." However, O'Keefe didn't stop with this outlandish story. He built a stone grave near the weather station with a marker that read: "Erected in Memory of Erin O'Keefe, Daughter of John and Nora O'Keefe, Who Was Eaten by Mountain Rats in the Year 1876."

The story spread across the country and a New York newspaper ran a woodcut that showed a swarm of sheep-sized rats crowded around a building topped with the stars and stripes. Foreign presses in England, Scotland and Ireland took it up and from there the story made it to the Continent.

O'Keefe went on to create other wild stories for the next few years. The army was not impressed with the old frontier stories that joshed the tenderfoot, and in 1881 O'Keefe was transferred to be "chief mule driver" of a burro train. His prolific imagination was not part of the job description and O'Keefe was destined for furlough. (a polite term for put out to pasture).

From this job, he was demoted to mucking out the mules' stalls. O'Keefe read the signs of how his career was headed, so he resigned and went on to become a fireman for the city of Denver. It certainly wasn't rampaging rats that ended his life—in 1895 when he was 38 years of age, he choked to death on a sip of tea in his home.

Can you still find the grave of Erin O'Keefe if you travel by car or the cog railway to the summit of Pikes Peak? Don't spend time crawling over the rubble there. The grave marker was stolen in the 1930s. Somewhere, there is a family with this "historical" artifact. Do you think the story behind it has survived with it? Or, is there some bemused descendent of the marker thief wondering what to do with this object?

Since one definition of a legend is "a lie that has attained the dignity of age," might one day, this legend resurface as supposed fact?

*This story was widely circulated in the 19th century.*

*Excerpted from* Storytelling Process and Practice *by Norma J. Livo and Sandra A Rietz, Libraries Unlimited, 1986.*

# *Coyote Goes Swimming*

(Montana, United States)

*Coyotes hate water. Not just a little bit, but with an abiding hatred. We lived in Montana and had become close friends with the manager of a large ranch nearby. This fourteen thousand acre cattlesheep spread and its manager were favorites of ours to visit.*

*One hot summer day we gathered up the kids and dog, and visited him. He took us around to show us many wonderful things. Among them was an Indian burial boulder at a remote spot on the ranch. There were all sorts of beads and artifacts that had fallen from bodies placed on the top of the rock. We saw hawks and in fact, we were chased off by a hawk when we got too close to her nest. She protected her chicks with fury and determination as she flew at us and swooped away to attack again.*

*However, it was the story our friend told us that was truly amazing.*

"One day I was out riding the fence line and I came to the top of a hill," he started. "I spotted a coyote down below doing something peculiar. The coyote was going along the fence and through my binoculars I saw the coyote gathering bits of sheep fleece that had been caught in the fence barbs."

He stopped to light his pipe and then continued. "The coyote gathered these bits of fleece and held them in his muzzle. Then the coyote trotted off to the lake below and to my amazement, the coyote slowly waded into the water."

"I want you city folks to realize that this is not coyote behavior," he said as he pointed the stem of his pipe at us. "The coyote waded until he had covered all of his body with water and then he swam out further. Finally, the only thing I could see was the white blob of fleece above the water. After a while, the coyote left the fleece floating and swam back to shore. He shook himself, rolled around on the ground and then trotted off."

Our friend squinted into the fading sun and continued, "I couldn't stand this mystery! Coyotes don't swim! So, I rode down to the lake and got off my horse on the shoreline. I gathered a big cottonwood branch from the nearby tree and fished the fleece out. It was easy to snag with the branch and I dragged it up to the shore. I hunkered down to examine it and was surprised to see that it was covered with fleas. That wily coyote had his own method of pest extermination."

Just as he said this, we heard the howl of several coyotes in the distance. I wonder if one of them knew how to control pest-some fleas?

# *Riddles, Verses, Rhymes, and Songs*

*I have an apple I can't cut,*
*A blanket I can't fold,*
*And so much money I can't count it.*

*(The sun, the moon and the stars)*

# *Questions*

(Asia)

Long ago, in a village far removed from anywhere else, an old man asked a little boy a teasing question. "In this great, giant land of ours, which is closer, the capital of our land or the sun?"

The boy answered without hesitation, "The sun of course."

"Well, and well," said the old man, smiling at the little boy. "And why do you say the sun?"

"That's easy," said the boy. "We can see the sun from right here, where we are, but we can't see our capital."

The aged man thought the boy exceedingly clever with his answer. The next day he asked the young boy to accompany him as he went to the marketplace to show off this young thinker to everyone he met there. Throngs of people from the capital passed through this small village, for it was on a main road to anywhere. The old man and the boy stood under a tree in the shade, and the old man pointed out this one and that one from afar, while the boy stared with an open mouth at the strange and beautiful clothing of the people that he saw.

"Now then," said the old man, when he saw that a goodly crowd of people had gathered around them under the tree. "Tell us, my little friend, which is closer, the capital or the sun?"

Again, the boy answered the question promptly, "The capital of course."

The old man's mouth sagged with disappointment. "But my lad, only yesterday you told me the sun was closer."

"Yes," said the boy. "But that was before we saw all these people from the capital. Have you ever seen anyone who came from the sun?"

# *The Frozen Logger*

(United States)

*As I stepped out one evening in a timber town café,*
*A six-foot seven waitress to me these words did say:*

*I see that you are a logger and not just a common bum*
*For nobody but a logger stirs his coffee with his thumb.*

*My lover was a logger. There's none like him today,*
*If you'd pour whiskey on it he would eat a bale of hay.*

*He never shaved a whisker from off his horney hide,*
*He'd just pound them in with a hammer and bite them off inside.*

*My lover came to see me one cold and wintry day,*
*He held me in a fond embrace that broke three vertebrae.*

*He kissed me when we parted, so hard it broke my jaw,*
*I could not speak to tell him he'd forgot his mackinaw.*

*I watched my lover leaving, a-sauntering through the snow,*
*Going gaily homeward at forty-eight below.*

*The weather it tried to freeze him. It tried its level best,*
*At one thousand degrees below zero, it froze up my logger love.*

*They tried in vain to thaw him, and if you'll believe me sir,*
*They made him into axe blades to chop the Douglas Fir.*

*And so I lost my lover and to this café I've come,*
*And here I'll wait till someone stirs his coffee with his thumb.*

# *Poor Old Woman*

(England)

*This silly little diddy has entertained children for generations.*

*There was an old woman who swallowed a fly,*
*Oh, my! Swallowed a fly!*
*Poor old woman, I think she'll die.*

*There was an old woman who swallowed a spider,*
*Right down inside her she swallowed a spider,*
*She swallowed the spider to kill the fly.*
*Oh, my! Swallowed a fly!*
*Poor old woman, I think she'll die.*

*There was an old woman who swallowed a bird,*
*How absurd to swallow a bird!*
*She swallowed the bird to kill the spider,*
*She swallowed the spider to kill the fly.*
*Oh, my! Swallowed a fly!*
*Poor old woman, I think she'll die.*

*There was an old woman who swallowed a cat,*
*Fancy that! She swallowed a cat!*
*She swallowed the cat to kill the bird,*
*She swallowed the bird to kill the spider,*
*She swallowed the spider to kill the fly.*
*Oh, my! Swallowed a fly!*
*Poor old woman, I think she'll die.*

*There was an old woman who swallowed a dog.*
*She swallowed the dog to kill the cat,*
*She swallowed the cat to kill the bird,*
*She swallowed the bird to kill the spider,*

*She swallowed the spider to kill the fly.*
*Oh, my! Swallowed a fly!*
*Poor old woman, I think she'll die.*

*There was an old woman who swallowed a cow,*
*I don't know how, but she swallowed a cow!*
*She swallowed the cow to kill the dog,*
*She swallowed the dog to kill the cat,*
*She swallowed the cat to kill the bird,*
*She swallowed the bird to kill the spider,*
*She swallowed the spider to kill the fly.*
*Oh, my! Swallowed a fly!*
*Poor old woman, I think she'll die.*

*There was an old woman who swallowed a horse!*
*She died, of course.*

# *The Owl and the Pussy-Cat*

(England)

*The Owl and the Pussy-Cat went to sea*
*In a beautiful pea-green boat:*
*They took some honey, and plenty of money*
*Wrapped up in a five-pound note.*
*The Owl looked up to the stars above,*
*And sang to a small guitar,*
*"O lovely Pussy, O Pussy, my love,*
*What a beautiful Pussy you are,*
*You are,*
*You are!*
*What a beautiful Pussy you are!"*

*Pussy said to the Owl, "You elegant fowl,*
*How charmingly sweet you sing!*
*Oh! let us be married; too long we have tarried,*
*But what shall we do for a ring?"*
*They sailed away, for a year and a day,*
*To the land where the bong-tree grows,*
*And there in a wood a Piggy-wig stood,*
*With a ring at the end of his nose,*
*His nose,*
*His nose,*
*With a ring at the end of his nose.*

*"Dear Pig, are you willing to sell for one shilling*
*Your ring?" said the Piggy, "I will."*
*So they took it away, and were married next day,*
*By the Turkey who lives on the hill.*
*They dined on mince and slices of quince,*
*Which they ate with a runcible spoon,*
*And hand in hand, on the edge of the sand,*
*They danced by the light of the moon,*
*The moon,*
*The moon,*
*They danced by the light of the moon.*

*A delightful 19th century verse from artist Edward Lear. Edward Lear, born in 1812, was the youngest of twenty-one children. He became an artist through painting birds and illustrating the works of naturalists. Lear was a landscape artist and traveled widely to paint. His Book of Nonsense, 1846, provided joy and fun to readers and listeners. Not only did he draw and paint, but taught as well, and Queen Victoria was among his students. He died in 1888.*

# *A Riddling Tale*

(Austria)

Three women were changed into flowers that grew in the field. One of the women was allowed to be in her own home at night. Once when day was drawing near, and she was forced to go back to her companions in the field and become a flower again, she said to her husband, "If you will come this afternoon and gather me, I shall be free and henceforth stay with you."

He did just as she had asked him to do.

Now, the question is: how did her husband know her for the flowers were exactly alike. There were no differences among them.

Answer: Since she was at her home during the night and not in the field, no dew fell on her as it did on the others, and by this her husband knew which of the flowers was his wife.

# *Riddle Song*

(Unknown)

*I brought my love a cherry that has no stone,*
*I brought my love a chicken that has no bone,*
*I told my love a story that has no end,*
*I brought my love a baby and no cryen*

*How can there be a cherry that has no stone?*
*How can there be a chicken that has no bone?*
*How can there be a story that has no end?*
*How can there be a baby and no cryen?*

*A cherry when it's blooming it has no stone,*
*A chicken in the egg it has no bone,*
*The story of our love shall have no end,*
*A baby when it's sleeping there's no cryen.*

*The source and date of origin of this ancient riddle song are unknown.*

# *A Visit from St. Nicholas*

(United States)

*'Twas the night before Christmas, when all through the house,*
*Not a creature was stirring, not even a mouse.*
*The stockings were hung by the chimney with care,*
*In hopes that St. Nicholas soon would be there.*
*The children were nestled all snug in their beds,*
*While visions of sugar-plums danced in their heads,*
*And mamma in her kerchief, and I in my cap,*
*Had just settled our brains for a long winter's nap.*
*When out on the lawn there arose such a clatter,*
*I sprang from my bed to see what was the matter.*
*Away to the window I flew like a flash,*
*Tore open the shutter, and threw up the sash.*
*The moon on the breast of the new-fallen snow,*
*Gave a lustre of midday to objects below;*
*When what to my wondering eyes should appear?*
*But a miniature sleigh and eight tiny reindeer,*
*With a little old driver, so lively and quick,*
*I knew in a moment it must be St. Nick!*
*More rapid than eagles his coursers they came,*
*And he whistled and shouted and called them by name.*
*"Now, Dasher! now, Dancer! now, Prancer and Vixen!*
*On, Comet! on Cupid! on Donder and Blitzen!*
*To the top of the porch, to the top of the wall,*
*Now, dash away, dash away, dash away all!"*

*As dry leaves that before the wild hurricane fly,*
*When they meet with an obstacle mount to the sky,*
*So, up to the housetop the coursers they flew,*
*With a sleigh full of toys, and St. Nicholas, too,*
*And then, in a twinkling, I heard on the roof*
*The prancing and pawing of each little hoof.*
*As I drew in my head and was turning around,*
*Down the chimney St. Nicholas came with a bound:*
*He was dressed all in fur from his head to his foot,*
*And his clothes were all tarnished with ashes and soot,*
*A bundle of toys he had flung on his back,*
*And he looked like a peddler just opening his pack.*
*His eyes, how they twinkled! his dimples; how merry!*
*His cheeks were like roses, his nose like a cherry;*
*His droll little mouth was drawn up like a bow,*
*And the beard on his chin was as white as the snow.*
*The stump of a pipe he held tight in his teeth,*
*And the smoke, it encircled his head like a wreath.*
*He had a broad face and a little round belly,*
*That shook, when he laughed, like a bowl full of jelly.*
*He was chubby and plump, a right jolly old elf;*
*A wink of his eye, and a twist of his head,*
*Soon gave me to know I had nothing to dread.*
*He spoke not a word, but went straight to his work,*
*And filled all the stockings: then turned with a jerk.*
*And laying his finger aside of his nose,*
*And giving a nod, up the chimney he rose.*
*He sprang to his sleigh, to his team gave a whistle,*
*And away they all flew like the down of a thistle.*
*But I heard him exclaim, ere he drove out of sight,*
*"Happy Christmas to all, and to all a good-night!"*

*This poem, written in the early 19th century by Clement C. Moore, has delighted many generations of children. Clement C. Moore was born in New York in 1779. He graduated from Columbia and held the chair of Biblical learning at the Theological Seminary of New York. He died in 1863.His poem, A Visit from St. Nicholas, has become part of the American tradition of Christmas. It appeared on the 23rd of December, 1823, anonymously in the New York Troy Sentinel. It had been written for his family and has gone on to gain lasting merit.*

# *The Shepherd Boy*

(Eastern Europe)

Once upon a time, there was a shepherd boy whose fame spread far and wide because of the wise answers he gave to every question. The King of the country heard of it likewise, but did not believe it. He sent for the boy.

The King asked the boy, "If you can give me an answer to three questions which I will ask you, I will look on you as my own child. You shall dwell with me in my royal palace."

"What are the three questions?" the boy asked.

The king said, "The first is, how many drops of water are there in the ocean?"

The shepherd boy needed no time to think about it. He answered, "Lord King, if you will have all the rivers on earth dammed up so that not a single drop runs from them into the sea until I have counted it, I will tell you how many drops there are in the sea."

The King's brows went up, he stroked the beard on his chin and said, "The next question is, how many stars are there in the sky?"

Without even the slightest frown, the shepherd boy said, "Give me a great sheet of white paper." Then he made so many fine points on it with a pen that they could scarcely be seen, and it was all but impossible to count them. Any one who looked at them would have lost his sight. Then the shepherd boy quietly said, "There are as many stars in the sky as there are points on the paper. Just count them." But of course, no one was able to do it.

The King, looking puzzled, now asked, "The third question is, how many seconds of time are there in eternity?"

Quickly the shepherd boy replied, "In Lower Pomerania is the Diamond Mountain, which is two miles and a half high, two miles and a half wide, and two miles and a half deep. Every hundred years a little bird comes and sharpens its beak on it and when the whole mountain is worn away by this, then the first second of eternity will be over."

The King then announced to everyone present and the little shepherd boy, "You have answered the three questions like a wise man, and you shall henceforth dwell with me in my royal palace, and I will regard you as my own child."

# A Collection of Short Riddles

(Unknown)

*On yonder hill there is a red deer,*
*The more you shoot, the more you may,*
*You cannot drive that deer away.*

*(Ancient riddle: the sun rising.)*

*In spring I look gay,*
*Deck'd in comely array,*
*In summer more clothing I wear,*
*When colder it grows,*
*I fling off my clothes,*
*And in winter quite naked appear.*

*(Deciduous tree)*

*Thirty white horses upon a red hill,*
*Now they champ, now they stamp,*
*Now they stand still.*

*(Teeth)*

*Round the house and round the house,*
*And there lies a white glove in the window.*

*(Snow)*

*A hill full, a hole full,*
*But you cannot catch a bowlful.*

*(Smoke)*

*From house to house he goes,*
*So sure and yet so slight,*
*And whether it rains or snows,*
*He sleeps outside all night.*

*(A lane)*

*Jack-at-a-word ran over the moor,*
*Never behind but always before.*

*(Will-o-the-wisp)*

*What flies forever*
*And rests never?*

*(Wind)*

*The more you feed it,*
*The more it'll grow high,*
*But if you give it water,*
*Then it'll go and die.*

*(Fire)*

*I washed my face in water,*
*That neither rained nor run.*
*I dried my face on a towel,*
*That was neither wove nor spun.*

*(Dew and Sun)*

*White bird, featherless,*
*Flew from Paradise,*
*Pitched on the castle wall.*
*Poor Lord Landless,*
*Came in a fine dress,*
*And went away without a dress at all.*

*(Snow)*

# *Bibliography*


Applebaum, David, ed. "The Fool." *Parabola* 26(3), Fall 2001.

Bancroft, Caroline. *Two Burros of Fairplay*. Boulder: Johnson Publishing Company, 1968.

Bryant, Sara Cone. *Epaminondas and His Auntie*. Boston: Houghton Mifflin Co., 1938.

Chase, Mary. *Harvey*. Dramatists Play Service, Inc., New York, 1970.

Cousins, Norman. *Anatomy of an Illness as Perceived by the Patient*. New York: W.W. Norton, 1979.

Demi. *The Dragon's Tale*. New York: Henry Holt and Company, 1996.

Getlen, Larry, ed. *The Complete Idiot's Guide to Jokes*. Indianapolis: Alpha Publishers, 2006.

Huang, Chungliang Al. *The Chinese Book of Animal Powers*. New York: HarperCollins, 1999.

Hazlitt, W. Carew. *Merry Tales of the Mad Men of Gotham*. Publisher unknown. 1620 edition.

Jacobs, Joseph. *English Fairy Tales*. New York: Putnam, 1892.

Jagendorf, M.A. *The Merry Men of Gotham*. New York: Vanguard Press, 1950.

Jagendorf, M.A. *Tyll Ulenspiegel's Merry Pranks*. New York: Vanguard Press, 1938.

Kimmel, Eric A. *The Rooster's Antlers*. New York: Holiday House, 1999.

Livo, Norma J. *Troubadour's Storybag*. Golden: Fulcrum, 1996.

———. *Story Medicine*. Englewood: Libraries Unlimited, 2001.

———, Guest Editor. "Storytelling and Humor." *Storytelling Magazine*. Jonesborough: National Storytelling Network, 2003.

———, and Dia Cha. *Folk Stories of the Hmong*. Westport: Libraries Unlimited, 1991.

———, and Sandra Rietz. *Storytelling Process and Practice*. Littleton: Libraries Unlimited, 1986.

Merriam, Eve. *Epaminondas*, illustrated by Trina Schart Hyman. Chicago: Follett Publishing, 1968.

Rice, James, illus. *Cajun Night Before Christmas*, edited by Howard Jacobs. Gretna: Pelican Publishers, 1973.

———, illus. *Hillbilly Night Afore Christmas*. Gretna: Pelican Publishers, 1983.

———. *Cowboy Night Before Christmas*. Gretna: Pelican Publishers, 1986.

Schwartz, Alvin. *Tomfoolery: Trickery and Foolery With Words*. New York: Lippincott, 1973.

———. *Whoppers: Tall Tales and Other Lies*. New York: Lippincott, 1975.

———. *Kickle Snifters and Other Fearsome Critters*. New York: Lippincott, 1976.

———. *Flapdoodle: Pure Nonsense From American Folklore*. New York: Lippincott, 1980.

———. *Tales of Trickery from the Land of Spoof*. New York: Farrar, Straus and Giroux, 1985.

Singer, Isaac Bashevis. *The Fools of Chelm*, illustrated by Uri Schulvitz. New York: Farrar, Straus and Giroux, 1973.

Stapleton, Alfred. *All About the Merry Tales of Gotham*, illustrated by Harry Packer. London: Kessinger, 2005.

Thurber, James. "The Secret Life of Walter Mitty." *James Thurber: Writings and Drawings*. New York: Literary Classics of the U.S., Inc., Library of America Series, 1996. (This was first published in 1941 and can be found in many anthologies.)

Tidwell, James S., ed. *The Treasury of American Folk Humor*. New York: Bonanza Books, 1956.

Wigginton, Eliot, ed. *Foxfire Books 1-8*. Mountain City: The Foxfire Fund, Inc., 1966–1984.

Yolan, Jane. *Sleeping Ugly*, illustrated by Jane Stanley. New York: Coward McCann, 1981.

Young, Ed. *Cat and Rat*. New York: Henry Holt and Co., 1995.
Yuan, Haiwang. *The Magic Lotus Lantern and Other Tales from the Han Chinese*. Westport: Libraries Unlimited, 2006.

## INTERNET SOURCES

Association for Applied and Therapeutic Humor. http://www.aath.org.
Humor Matters. http://www.humormatters.com.
The Humor Project. http://www.humorproject.com.
Klein, Allen. The Jollytologist. http://www.allenklein.com.
Laughter Yoga. http://www.laughteryoga.org/. (Contains information on this new revolution in body–mind medicine that combines simple laughter exercises and gentle yoga breathing to enhance health and happiness.)
Sheppard, Tim. Humorous Storytelling. http://www.timsheppard.co.uk/story/dir/humorous.html.
World Laughter Tour. www.worldlaughtertour.com.

## VHS AND DVD MATERIALS

*Bob Hope, The Road to Laughter*, VHS, directed by David Leaf and John Scheinfeld. New York: Hart Sharp Video, 2003.
*Red Skelton, King of Laughter*, DVD. Wallingford: Good Times Video, 2001.
*The Three Stooges: Kings of Laughter*, DVD. Wallingford: Good Times Video, 2001.

# *Appreciation*

I end this book with deepest appreciation to Barbara Ittner, who was an astute, discriminating, gentle, supportive, and wise reader and reactor to this book, as well as a friend over many years. Many thanks.

# *Index*

# About the Author

Norma J. Livo grew up in a rich time of no television and in a rich place—the hills of Pennsylvania. It was there that she heard many stories and songs told and played by family and

Photographs by Stephen Wilcox and Lauren Livo

These two modes of transportation of the author are separated by over 70 years and many stories. Of course, both of the stories behind these pictures contain humor.

community members at regular gatherings. "Let's Pretend," broadcast on Saturday mornings on the radio was also a highpoint for her. Many of these stories, she heard, learned, and learned to tell, over three-quarters of a century. Each of them still reverberate significant memories.

Norma left home to get a doctorate from the University of Pittsburgh. She became a teacher and professor, as well as a believer that the oral literature of her childhood was crucial to teaching and learning. She joined and eventually served on the Board of Directors of the National Association for the Preservation and Perpetuation of Storytelling (NAPPS). She also founded the Rocky Mountain Storytelling Conference.

Norma's amazing family (husband, four children, their spouses, and seven grandchildren) has been important in her journey to preserve and perpetuate stories and the traditions of storytelling. She has written and co-authored numerous books, including a storytelling textbook. Her work has received critical acclaim as well as awards from the National Storytelling Network and the Colorado Author's League. In 2002, Norma was honored with NSN's ORACLE Award for Lifetime Achievement. In addition to her many professional accomplishments, Norma is a private pilot and a nature lover. To her, life has been just one story after another.